DAN SUELZLE

HARVEST HOUSE PUBLISHERS
EUGENE, OREGON

Cover design by Brian Bobel Design

Misquoted
Copyright © 2019 by Dan Suelzle
Published by Harvest House Publishers
Eugene, Oregon 97408
www.harvesthousepublishers.com

ISBN 978-0-7369-7482-0 (pbk.)
ISBN 978-0-7369-7483-7 (eBook)

Library of Congress Cataloging-in-Publication Data

Names: Suelzle, Dan, 1984- author.
Title: Misquoted / Dan Suelzle.
Description: Eugene : Harvest House Publishers, 2019.
Identifiers: LCCN 2019004514 (print) | LCCN 2019005514 (ebook) | ISBN
    9780736974837 (ebook) | ISBN 9780736974820 (pbk.)
Subjects: LCSH: Bible--Criticism, interpretation, etc.
Classification: LCC BS511.3 (ebook) | LCC BS511.3 .S838 2019 (print) | DDC
    220.6--dc23
LC record available at https://lccn.loc.gov/2019004514

Printed in the United States of America

19 20 21 22 23 24 25 26 27 / BP-GL / 10 9 8 7 6 5 4 3 2 1

To my parents, who taught me the Faith
that was delivered once for all to the saints.

Acknowledgments

Thanks are in order when any book is published, on account of the many hands that work to bring it to fruition, the eyes that read its many drafts, and the meandering conversations that the process evokes.

I owe my thanks first to Harvest House Publishers for this opportunity. Kathleen Kerr and Terry Glaspey have been especially patient and helpful in the process and I have valued their encouragement.

I also greatly appreciate the time invested by those friends, family members, and colleagues who read the manuscript—either in bits or in its entirety—and subsequently offered suggestions and insights that have made the book better than it would have been otherwise.

Contents

" Introduction "

The Bible is not about you.

Blessed are you if that statement does not offend you. I wrote the thing and it still gets under my skin. But it's true. As much as we do not want it to be the case, the Bible is not about you or me. It's likely that you have heard preaching and teaching to the contrary. I certainly have. And frankly it's kind of nice. After all, I like to hear about me. I suspect you like to hear about you too. How special God thinks you are. How necessary you are to his plan. How he has great things in store for you. How he wants you to have an abundant life, full of many earthly blessings. How everything that happens in your life has some divine reason undergirding it. How you have a unique purpose on this earth and all you have to do is discover it and everything in life will fall perfectly into place. I have heard all of that and more. And I like it. It's tempting. It's flattering. It's exciting.

And it is dead wrong.

Now, please stick with me. I certainly do not mean to discourage you right from the start. I do not mean to say that the Bible has nothing to say to you. But I do want to show you that,

precisely because you are *not* at the center of the Bible, it is actually wonderfully good news; liberating news; news that forgives,
renews, and strengthens you in the one true faith. I want to show
you how the Bible is about Jesus for you. If that doesn't sound
terribly revolutionary to you, good. But the state of preaching
and teaching in Christ's church these days has unfortunately—
and ironically—made such a statement sound strange to many
Christian ears. We should rejoice that the Bible is about Jesus
for us, and yet so often what pulpits, Bible studies, and airwaves
give us is a terribly narcissistic—and comfortless—faith.

But when you realize that the Bible is all about Jesus for
you—how the promises of Jesus emanate from every page; how
the truth of Christ stands firm even apart from you—then the
Scriptures become an ever-flowing fountain and source of true
hope and lasting comfort. This book aims to show precisely that,
by dealing with commonly misquoted verses from God's Word.

Context, Context, Context

Misquoting the Bible is really quite simple. All you have
to do is ignore the context of any given verse. "Bible scrab-
ble" is how one parishioner described it. Take a piece of a verse
from here, a couple words from that verse over there, mash
them together, and you have a teaching that is "from the
Bible," but is as far from biblical as you can get: "Solomon had
700 wives…and 300 concubines…You go, and do likewise"
(1 Kings 11:3; Luke 10:37). One of my New Testament college
professors put it like this: "A Bible text without a context is a
pretext for a prooftext." Yeah. Read that one again. Put another
way, when a text is divorced from its context, it is probably

because a person is simply looking for a verse to reinforce what he already thinks. It is a reversal of fit: rather than having his mind shaped and reformed by the Scriptures, he would rather shape and form the Scriptures to fit his whims and conform to human wisdom. It's simple: if you want to misuse God's Word, then quote as little of God's Word as possible. You will be able to make God say anything you please. And he will probably sound a lot like you.

However, if misquoting the Bible is simple, the solution is equally so. I have heard countless debates and discussions about the Bible that basically end up at an impasse. It becomes one person's interpretation versus another's. "Well, what that means *to me* is..." But should we really be concerned about what the Bible means *to me*? Shouldn't we care simply about what it *means*? What the Bible means and what it means *to me* should not be two different things—at least if we are truly committed to rejoicing in the truth. I am convinced that the vast majority of the Bible does not need to be interpreted. It just needs to be read on its own terms, *in context*. To be sure, there are confusing, mysterious parts of the Bible that have elicited many and varied interpretations. There are parts of the Bible where all we can say is, "It seems to be saying this..." or "I'm not sure. Perhaps he meant that..." With such verses, multiple interpretations are unavoidable, and there are different perspectives to be considered. Even so, we should always let the clear passages of the Bible lead the charge in interpreting the unclear ones, so as never to make the Bible fight against itself.

When you pick up a newspaper, you intuitively know how to read it. You do not go to the comics section searching for weather forecasts. You do not look in the obituaries to try to find the score of last night's ball game. The front-page headline story is likely going to be of a different flavor than the letters to the editor in the opinion section. Without even thinking about it, you read the newspaper on its own terms, in its context, and according to its various genres.

In many ways the Bible is no different. It is a library of understandable documents, made up of paragraphs, sentences, words, letters, grammar, syntax, verbs, subjects, objects, and prepositions that all work together to communicate something. Some of the documents are historical narratives that simply convey a story from the past. Some of them contain genealogical records (great devotional material, that is). Some of them are poetic hymns of doxological praise, prayers in the midst of suffering, or small nuggets of earthly wisdom. Some of the documents show how God has fulfilled his promises of old, others proclaim what is yet to come, and still others teach what God's people should do and believe in the meantime. There are multiple literary genres contained in the Bible, and here's the point: each one needs to be read on its own terms and in its own context. This is the first step in rightly understanding the Bible. But the goal of reading and studying the Bible is much greater than delivering mere historical facts.

So That You May Believe

Near the end of his Gospel, the apostle John reports exactly why he has recorded the events of Jesus's ministry: "These are written so that you may believe that Jesus is the Christ, the Son of God, and that by believing you may have life in his name"

(John 20:31). Here we are told that the purpose of John's Gospel is not simply to convey historical information, although it certainly does that. John also does not record the ministry of Jesus, the Lamb of God, as self-help encouragement to stick in your back pocket that will get you through the day when the world has got you down. Rather, John would have you hear of the mighty works of Jesus, so that you would believe him to be the promised Messiah in whom all the promises of God are fulfilled, *and* that by believing you would have life in the name of Jesus, apart from whom salvation cannot be found (Acts 4:12).

Jesus makes such a claim about himself more than once in the Bible. For example, consider the time that Jesus teaches the Jews in John 5:24. He gives them the promise that "whoever hears my word and believes him who sent me has eternal life. He does not come into judgment, but has passed from death to life." That sounds like a pretty good promise, like a word worth hearing and believing. And yet a little later he says, "You search the Scriptures because you think that in them you have eternal life; *and it is they that bear witness about me*, yet you refuse to come to me that you may have life" (vv. 39-40). Jesus claims that he is the fulfillment of the Scriptures, and that is precisely the stumbling block for the Jews to whom he speaks.

In Luke 4:16-21 a similar thing happens. In a scene that has you on the edge of your seat, Jesus reads from the scroll of Isaiah, chapter 61. When he is done, he sits down. All eyes are on him, waiting for him to speak, when he remarkably declares, "Today this Scripture has been fulfilled in your hearing." He claims that he is the one about whom Isaiah wrote some eight centuries earlier.

Or do you remember the first Easter when Jesus meets the Emmaus disciples (Luke 24:13-27)? He acts as if he does not know what has just happened in Jerusalem. They sadly—and ironically—inform him of his own crucifixion. And notice his response: "'O foolish ones, and slow of heart to believe *all that the prophets have spoken*! Was it not necessary that the Christ should suffer these things and enter into his glory?' And beginning with Moses and all the Prophets, he interpreted to them in all the Scriptures *the things concerning himself*" (vv. 25-27).

Here is the point: the Bible is not about you. It is about Jesus for you. Jesus says so himself. All of the Scriptures point to Jesus. The purpose of the Bible is to give you Jesus, so that you would have true, eternal resurrection life through the forgiveness of your sins.

Comfort Reclaimed

The point of this book, then, is not merely to learn information about the Bible and its contents—although that is certainly not unimportant. The point is not to have all the right answers for any theological debate that may arise—although the Bible does exhort us to be prepared in all seasons to give a reasoned defense for the hope that is within us (1 Peter 3:15). The point is not so that you can piecemeal together your own belief system that suits your own desires.

No, the goal of this book is to help you better understand the overarching story of the Scriptures, with Christ as the center, so that by them you would be given true comfort in the midst of the suffering, doubts, and sin that you will experience in this life. One of my favorite prayers captures it well:

> Blessed Lord, You have caused all Holy Scriptures to
> be written for our learning. Grant that we may so hear
> them, read, mark, learn, and take them to heart that,
> by the patience and comfort of Your holy Word, we
> may embrace and ever hold fast the blessed hope of
> everlasting life; through Jesus Christ, Your Son, our
> Lord, who lives and reigns with You and the Holy
> Spirit, one God, now and forever. Amen.[1]

We receive God's Word into our entire being—we hear, read,
mark, learn, and take it to heart—because there we are shown
the only hope worth clinging to, the only hope that is truly
hope. It is not mere wishful thinking, but the promise of life
everlasting, where suffering, doubt, and sin will finally be no
more. That future promise has a way of giving us present comfort in the midst of all manner of suffering.

A Final Note and an Exhortation

I have often said that it is naïve to think that a person can
read the Bible objectively, without any kind of bias. Everyone brings assumptions and presuppositions to the study of
the Scriptures, including me. I pray that where my presuppositions are proven wrong by God's Word, he would grant
me repentance, so that I would rejoice all the more in his truth
alone.

In the interest of full disclosure, I am a Lutheran pastor,
ordained in the Lutheran Church—Missouri Synod *(www
.lcms.org)*. I have publicly vowed that I subscribe without res-
ervation to the Scriptures and their exposition as contained
in the Book of Concord (1580). As a result, I bring Lutheran

presuppositions to the text when I study it. With every text I read, I presuppose that:

- The Bible is God's sufficient, understandable, self-revelation to mankind.

- As God's Word, the Bible is inerrant and infallible, and therefore cannot lead into error, falsehood, or unbelief (John 17:17).

- As God's Word, the Bible is efficacious. That is, it actually delivers salvation and forgiveness of sin in its very proclamation (Romans 10:17; 1 Corinthians 1:22-24).

- Where God's Word contradicts my reason or experience, it is my job to submit to the text, not to force the text to submit to me, even when I cannot fully comprehend all of its details (Romans 11:33; 1 Corinthians 1:25).

- Most importantly, the Bible is not about me. It is about Jesus for me. Therefore, I ask of every text, "Where is Christ?"

As a pastor, there have been occasions where simply teaching the truth of God given in the Bible has stolen comfort from the one hearing it. While certainly not enjoyable, such an experience is not necessarily bad. We all have a way of clinging to thoughts and feelings that may seem good and right but may indeed be proven false by God's Word. At the same time, I would hope that, over time, I have become better at replacing that false comfort with the true comfort of the pure gospel. I hope that if false comfort is taken from you in these pages, true and lasting comfort in Christ would always take its place. That is why each chapter is split up into three sections. First, I ask you to *Consider the Claim* that is made by some using a specific Bible verse. Second, we *Consider the Context* of that verse to determine if the claim being made is valid. Third, and most importantly, I have you *Consider the Comfort* that comes with a right, contextual understanding of the verse.

Authors, I think, are prone to a specific sort of temptation. Our words are chosen carefully. We write them, read them, mull them over, rewrite them, let them rest, and mull them over again. A sentence that takes the reader two seconds to read, may have taken twenty minutes to perfect. The temptation for authors, then, is to become unhealthily attached to our words and to use many of them. Why use five words when thirty-seven perfectly chosen ones will suffice?

When treating biblical texts especially, it seems there is always more to be said. I hope that I have said enough to treat each text sufficiently, but also not so much that you will become bogged down in words. Where that may have happened, I ask for your grace, and hope that by the end of the chapter the extra words will prove themselves worthwhile.

Finally, an exhortation. Concerning everything I say in this book, please do not simply take my word for any of it. It is your duty and privilege to compare what I say to God's Word, *in context*, and to let God's Word have its way, so that we would all be made wise unto salvation and grow up together into him who is the head: Jesus Christ our Lord.

Chapter 1

God Loves You Just the Way You Are

God is love.

1 JOHN 4:8

When I began my undergraduate studies, I enrolled at the University of North Dakota in Grand Forks. I was a music major studying vocal performance. Very quickly I also became involved with Campus Crusade for Christ (now known as Cru). In fact, my eighteen-month involvement with Cru, brief as it was, proved ironically invaluable for bolstering my Lutheran identity, though I would never have noticed it at the time.

During my freshman year on campus, Westboro Baptist Church announced they were coming to town. If you are not familiar with this group, do a quick internet search and you will quickly discover that they have firm convictions concerning the United States of America and the culture's despising of God's truth. Their methods are intensely polemic: trampling on the American flag, holding up signs that number the days that specific sinners have been burning in hell, picketing the funerals of dead service men and women, declaring that God hates this or that demographic of people, and the like.

Upon hearing the announcement that this group was going to be picketing on our campus, Cru launched into action organizing a counterprotest. The thinking was something along the lines of, "We can't have these kinds of people representing God and making the world think that all Christians are like this!" And so, armed with the conviction to represent Christ rightly to the world, we went on a noble campus crusade against these hateful people, and I joined right in. We were going to show them and the world that God is not hate, but God is love.

This was no small thing. We had the weighty responsibility of representing God himself, and doing so rightly. So, what does a group do to show the world how convicted they are about their noble and upright cause? What does a group do to get everyone's attention so that they can gain a hearing and proclaim God's overarching gospel truth that will save souls for all eternity?

They make T-shirts, of course.

You probably need only one guess to figure out what we had printed on the shirts. Three words, in big, red, bold print with the Bible reference on the back: GOD IS LOVE. This group came spouting hate, and so we were going to proclaim love. Decked out in our matching, cotton-blend, screen-printed, gospel-declaring armor, we marched into battle at the corner of University and Columbia where Westboro would fire the salvo.

The whole interaction was frankly rather lame. Westboro brought maybe fifteen people to hold signs and stand on flags. The Cru contingent was significantly larger, and there were some other student organizations that turned out in counter-protest. But it is not as though the whole city of Grand Forks— or even the majority of the campus—was there to watch the spectacle.

We would try to talk with the Westboro folks. Mostly they just ignored us and stood there, silently gripping their signs. A couple of times they would yell at us, but really it was a grand exercise in speaking past one another. They had their convictions, we had ours. They had their signs, we had our shirts. And neither was convincing the other of the superior truthfulness of their own position.

Ultimately, it was not the hard work of Cru that finally ended the whole thing. Ironically, it was only when the frat house across the street blared Springsteen's "Born in the USA" through their stereo that Westboro finally packed up their signs and went home. I guess Bruce had a way of saying things that eluded the piety of us Christians. We comforted and convinced ourselves of our victory with the typical, "Well, you never know how God will use the seeds we sowed."

Don't get me wrong. When the seed of God's Word is sown, he certainly does promise to make it grow according to his good pleasure (Isaiah 55:10-11). The problem is that we had not actually sown any seeds of God's Word in the first place. We had done precisely what this book aims to warn you against: we picked three words out of the Bible, ripped them out of context, slapped them on a shirt, and just repeated them over and over like some kind of magic spell, hoping that by mere repetition sinners would be turned from their errors. We kept spouting that "God is love," but we failed to explain what that meant—what God's love actually is, why we need it, or how we apprehend it.

There was one interaction on that street corner that I will never forget. I was standing next to a Westboro member trying to engage him in conversation. He was actually one of the calmer in the bunch, and I thought we might have a meaningful dialogue. As I tried to proclaim to him that "God is love" over and over, he finally looked me in the eye and calmly said, "Son, you apparently do not know what the love of God is."

Now, please do not hear me saying that Westboro Baptist Church had it right about the love of God. If you have ever heard them and seen their antics, God's love is a rare commodity, not because they proclaim God's wrath so polemically, but because they fail to proclaim the true gospel in its fullness. In any case, his comment stopped me in my tracks and forced me to think. It silenced my magical mantra and made me consider what I actually *meant* when I said, "God is love." Did I mean what the Bible taught? Had I—the son of a pastor and a faithful attender of church—failed all this time to understand what God's love is?

Consider the Claim

I would guess that if you asked most Christians in America from every denominational affiliation to tell you what the love of God is, they would likely answer in one of three ways.

First, some would describe God as a Hopeless Romantic. This version of God's love mimics our own human ideas about what love is. In this way of thinking, God's love consists of his great feelings for people. It is emotional love. It is gushy love. It is unconditional romantic love. If there is something that distinguishes such divine romantic love from human romantic love it is that God's love does not ebb and flow. His great feelings for people are constant and never wane. You can hear this version of God's love in many praise and worship songs where "God" or "Jesus" could be replaced with the name of your significant other and the song would unfortunately still make sense. Such songs are examples of how this romantic notion of God's love also has a way of instructing us about how we should reciprocate our love for him. The result is that our love for God is also considered to be nothing more than intense feelings that are qualitatively no different from the feelings we have for others. I love my friends, I love my siblings, I love my parents, I love my spouse and children. And I *really* love my God. Why? Because he *really* loves me.

The second popular perception of God and his love is God, the Hard-Nosed Father. This is the God of tough love. To this God, one must prove oneself. God is certainly loving, but you have to earn that love and show him that you are worthy of it. This is the God who raps the fingers of his students when they misbehave, but he does it because he loves them and the lesson they learn is worth the pain. This is the God who lays out his clear expectations and sets the bar high, not so that he can delight in your inevitable failure, but because he loves you so much that he wants to spur you on towards greatness. This is the God who will pay your college tuition and car loan as long as you maintain a 3.5 GPA. Whatever you do, you do not want to disappoint this God.

Finally, there is God, the Proud Grandparent. In the eyes of this God, you can do no wrong. If you happen to make a mistake, he overlooks it and focuses on the good qualities in you. This God is revealed in phrases like "God loves you just the way you are." This God is the one who is willing to redefine sin, to "look at the bright side" in it all, to chuckle and have you learn your lesson from it and put it behind you. This God does not want to call your sin what it is for fear that he may squash your self-esteem. He loves you, after all. And so instead, this God redefines sin as mere "growth areas"—opportunities to build you up and focus on your strengths.

Did you notice anything about those popular conceptions of God's love? They all have three things in common. First, they are all trying to deal with a problem: How is a person certain of God's love? How does a person apprehend this love and have a right standing in the sight of God? The answer to that question is the second commonality: all three of these perceptions of God's love give an answer to that problem that places the individual person at the center of everything. God's love ultimately is all about me. Either *I* am the unique center of God's affection, or *I* am the one who must work hard to earn his love and keep it, or *I* am the one he's always letting off the hook because his gleaming pride in *me* outweighs my mistakes. Finally, and most importantly, none of these popular conceptions of God's love require Jesus. None of them are unique to the God of the Bible.

When we turn to the Scriptures, we discover not only why

we need God's love, but also what God's love truly looks like and where it is to be found.

Consider the Context

The most popular and well-known verse that is quoted concerning the love of God is John 3:16. Some call it "The gospel in a nutshell." And why wouldn't we gravitate towards this verse? It has everything. It has God and his love, not only for some, but for the entire world. It has the language of sacrifice—a person giving up something of great value for the good of another. It speaks of faith and everlasting life. It is certainly full of God's love. However, it seems that this verse is often taught with God, the Hopeless Romantic in mind.

The ESV renders this verse: "For God so loved the world, that he gave his only Son, that whoever believes in him should not perish but have eternal life." Often the love of God here is considered to be quantitative: that God loved the world *so much* that he gave his one and only Son. The heart of God, the hopeless romantic, was just brimming over with so much affection for his creation that he couldn't help but save us. God is like the hero rushing in to save the damsel in distress. However, a closer look at the Greek helps us understand this verse better.

The key is in the word οὕτως (pronounced "HOO-tos"). It means "in this way" or "like this." So a bit more accurate translation of the Greek might be, "For God loved the world *like this*: he gave his one and only Son…" Such a translation asks us to consider *how* God loves the world, rather than *how much* God loves the world. *How* God loves the world is objective. It takes place in history. It is something outside of ourselves that we can point to and cling to in faith. *How much* God loves the world places God's love into the realm of the abstract and subjective. It is up to me to somehow peer into God's emotions to measure his love, and when I do that, God's love will inevitably start looking and sounding a lot like my own.

John 3:16 is so comforting precisely because it has the atoning work of Jesus as the objective proof of God's love for you and me.

Another popular text that speaks of God's love is Romans 5:8, "but God shows his love for us in that while we were still sinners, Christ died for us." This verse and its context shatter all ideas that God is a hard-nosed father who makes us earn his love. Consider Romans 5:6-7 to get a fuller understanding of verse 8: "For while we were still weak, at the right time Christ died for the ungodly. For one will scarcely die for a righteous person— though perhaps for a good person one would dare even to die— but God shows his love for us in that while we were still sinners, Christ died for us."

Notice how Paul here describes the recipients of God's love. He does not say that Christ dies for those really righteous people who have proven themselves worthy of such a gift. Paul does not say that Christ dies for people who are generally headed in the right direction and seeking after God. He does not even say that God's love is for people who are rather indifferent and neutral towards God. To the contrary, Paul says that God shows his love to his ungodly enemies. God's love is precisely for those who hate him. Those who want nothing to do with him. Those who sin against him and wish that he were nonexistent.

And yet, make no mistake. This does not mean that God is in the business of ignoring sin or pretending it does not exist. He is not a proud grandparent who simply overlooks the foibles of his beloved. God takes your sin so seriously that the only way to atone for it is to heap it upon his only begotten Son, Jesus Christ. And it kills him. In that death of Christ, you see God's true love, as his full wrath upon your own sin is poured out upon someone else. Only in Christ can your sin be fully judged *and* you are not destroyed in the process. As Paul says earlier in Romans 3, Jesus is the only means by which God can be both just in punishing sin *and* the one who justifies the sinner, making us pure, righteous, sinless (Romans 3:26). Martin Luther described it as the "happy exchange." Christ gets all that is yours: your sin, wretchedness, and enmity with God. In return, you receive all that is Christ's: righteousness and the favor of God.

When we consider God's love as an objective action that is fulfilled in Christ, then God's love becomes truly comforting. It no longer depends upon my earning it. Nor does it depend upon my own ideas or feelings of *how much* God loves me. The truth is that you cannot know or have the love of God apart from his Son, Jesus, who has objectively died and risen again to forgive your sins.

My Cru contingency and I were spouting like a mantra that "God is love" to speak out against the Westboro protestors. But the piece that we were leaving out was Jesus. Specifically, Jesus as the objective sacrifice for the sin of the world. As the very next verse in 1 John 4 says: "In this the love of God was made manifest among us, that God sent his only Son into the world, so that we might live through him." That objective reality of Christ crucified and risen brings comfort even in the valley of the shadow of death.

Consider the Comfort

I remember being at the bedside of a dying parishioner. Jeff had kidney failure, and the doctors said that his final breath was only a few days away. While we were talking, he became very upset and started crying. "I'm scared," he said. Of course, all sorts of things can scare a person as death draws near. Are they scared of the pain or of the unknown or of what might happen to the ones they leave behind?

"What is scaring you?" I asked.

"I am scared that I might not get to go to heaven."

Admittedly, my first instinct in that moment was to rush in with the gospel. To assure Jeff that when he died he would indeed be in the presence of his Savior. But to rush to the gospel would have been to rob it of its power. I first needed to know *why* he thought he was not going to attain eternal life.

After a little inquiry, Jeff said, "Pastor, you do not know the kind of life I have lived." That is all he needed to say for me to know the source of his fear. He had lived his life believing that God was no different than a hard-nosed father. Jeff had tried again and again to prove himself worthy of God's love, but he knew that he had come up short. Certainly, upon death, God was not going to be happy with his performance, and his fear was that he would be cast into hell as the heavenly Father shook his head in disappointment.

Knowing precisely where his fear of death was seated, what

a joy it was for me to proclaim to him a right, scriptural under-standing of the love of God in Christ. The worst thing I could have done in that moment would have been to speak about God as a proud grandparent. To say that everything is okay. That everyone makes mistakes in life and he should not be so hard on himself. Nor would it have been helpful to proclaim God the hopeless romantic with some vague idea of God's great love. That would have asked a dying man to peer into the abstract and vague emotions of God where certainty is nowhere to be found.

No, the first thing I told Jeff was that he was right. That he had not measured up to God's standard. That he had not lived as he should have. He had sinned against God, both in what he had done and in what he had left undone. He had vio-lated God's holy law in thought, word, and deed. There were no excuses, no extenuating circumstances that could get him off the hook. He was sinful and deserved hell because of it.

But I also got to proclaim to Jeff that that's not the end of the story.

The good news—which is all the sweeter when the sinful condition is taken seriously and properly diagnosed—is that God does not deal with you as your sin deserves. He deals with *Christ* as your sin deserves. That is the true love of God that the Scriptures give to you. I got to proclaim to Jeff from Romans 8 that even in the midst of terrible suffering and even in the face of death itself, there is nothing that can separate us from the love of God. But that love is not vague and formless. It has an objec-tive form and a shape *in Christ,* who has not only died, but has risen again, proving himself victorious over death and the grave. I got to proclaim to Jeff that because he was in Christ, his own death would not have the last word. There was no sin that he had committed or could commit that was too great for Christ's shed blood to cover.

Jeff died in faith the next day. He died knowing God's objective love in Christ. It will be good to see him when Christ returns in glory.

Chapter 2

Give Everything for Jesus

The kingdom of heaven is like treasure hidden in a field, which a man found and covered up. Then in his joy he goes and sells all that he has and buys that field. Again, the kingdom of heaven is like a merchant in search of fine pearls, who, on finding one pearl of great value, went and sold all that he had and bought it.

MATTHEW 13:44-46

Consider the Claim

Have you given everything?" It was the question posed by a speaker at a youth conference I attended. In his presentation he had crescendoed to this moment by having us consider all the things in our lives that we cling to and in which we find our identity. He talked about our materialistic culture that would have us cherish things like fashionable clothing, fancy cars, big houses, and a really good job to pay for it all. He talked about less concrete things like fame, popularity, and acceptance from our peers. He then spoke about how following Christ is costly business; how Christ asks us to give up many of the things we hold dear. And the climax was his question, "So what about you? Have you given everything? Have you given everything to follow Jesus?"

After posing the question and pausing for effect, he had us consider two pieces of Scripture to back up his teaching. The first was the story of the rich man in Luke 18:18-27. The second included the parables of the treasure and the pearl in Matthew 13:44-45. The rich man, he taught us, shows us that following Christ requires us to give everything, no matter how difficult that may be. We do not want to be like the rich man, who went away sad because he cherished his possessions more than being a Christ-follower. The parables of the treasure and the pearl, he said, are further examples of what the kingdom of God costs. It is so valuable that we should be glad to give up everything for it.

Now, I would never quibble with certain points of this man's teaching. To be sure, the gracious and saving reign and rule of Christ—the kingdom of God—is incredibly valuable. Indeed, it is impossible to think of anything more valuable. Also, being a part of Christ's reign as one of his disciples certainly carries a cost. Jesus promises as much to his apostles, and their subsequent deaths as martyrs prove his words to be true. It was not their deaths as martyrs that made the kingdom of heaven and eternal life theirs. Rather, they suffered because such things were *already* theirs, and they did so gladly (e.g. Acts 5:40).

Where I would quibble with this teacher, however, is how we

are incorporated into the reign and rule of Christ. Is it because of something we have done, or is it because of something Christ has done? As I sat there and listened to his very convicted—and convicting—preaching, I thought to myself, *Well, no. I guess if I'm honest I haven't given everything for the kingdom of God. I haven't given everything to become a disciple of Jesus.* But what did that even mean? After all, the guy who was preaching to us had on some pretty fashionable clothes. He was well-groomed. Presumably he lived in a comfortable house and his wedding ring indicated that he was at least married. Perhaps he even had children. He was not living a monastic life. Why did he make it sound like I should?

The question actually led me down two lines of thinking. The first was pride. I was willing to admit that I had not "given everything" to be a follower of Jesus. But I had at least given *some* things. I was willing to be a little bit unpopular at school because of confessing Jesus. And I also knew there were others in that room who had sacrificed much less to be Christian. They were only Christian on the outside. At least I was a real Christian, even if I was imperfect.

That prideful thinking, however, was quickly swallowed up by despair. *What if I'm wrong? What if I'm the only one in this room who hasn't given everything to follow Jesus? I don't want to look like a bad Christian. I'll just keep on pretending like I've got it all together.*

When preachers take the stage with questions like, "Have you given everything to follow Jesus?" they are in fact inviting us to ride the pendulum that swings between such pride and despair. Obviously the answer to that question for all of us, if we are honest, is no. And yet, in our sin, we like to think that the answer is a firm, "Well, I try pretty hard."

But Jesus does not grade on a curve. Either he requires that we give up everything to be a part of his kingdom—without exception—or else Jesus is saying something different in these texts than what this preacher was saying.

Consider the Context

The two texts that this teacher used, upon closer examination, are not saying what he wanted them to say. Let's look first at the account of the rich man.

In Luke 18:18 a ruler approaches Jesus and asks him, "Good Teacher, what must I do to inherit eternal life?" Immediately as readers we can glean some information about this man. First, his view of Jesus, while high, is not quite high enough. He views Jesus as a good teacher—and apparently nothing more. Jesus says as much when he notes the irony and responds, "Why do you call me good? No one is good except God alone."

Second, this man has a skewed idea of what it takes to inherit eternal life. The way he words the question betrays his misunderstanding. Inheritances, by their very nature, do not require the recipient to do anything. Any action that happens is solely on the part of the giver, and the action performed is to die. (As an aside, this is why it is such a slap in the face when the younger son asks his father for his share of the inheritance early in Luke 15:12. He may as well have said, "Hey, Dad, drop dead.")

So Jesus is dealing with a man who does not recognize his divine identity and who thinks that the gift of eternal life that Jesus brings is somehow earned by good works.

Now, Jesus could have answered, "What do you do to inherit eternal life? What a silly question! You don't do anything. I'm here to do it all for you." But that answer would have left this ruler blind to his sin and self-righteousness. So instead Jesus gives him a to-do list: "You know the commandments: 'Do not commit adultery, Do not murder, Do not steal, Do not bear false witness, Honor your father and mother'" (Luke 18:20).

If you have read Christ's sermon on the mount (Matthew 5–7), then you know that a simple exhortation to keep the commandments is not as easy as it sounds. He comes and ramps up these commandments. For example, Christ says that if you have even lusted after a woman in your heart, you are guilty of adultery, without ever having touched her. He says that if you even hate your brother in your heart, you are guilty of murder, without even having laid a hand on him. No one who looks back on their life can glibly say, "Oh, yeah. I've kept God's commandments. No problem." And yet this ruler does precisely that (Luke 18:21).

So Jesus has to ramp up the law for this man. Jesus has to tighten the noose of the law, as it were. He must show the ruler just how pitiful and wretched and blind he really is. Jesus has to show him the true status of his heart. So Jesus actually *adds* to the commandments to make his point: "One thing you still lack. Sell all that you have and distribute to the poor, and you will have treasure in heaven; and come, follow me" (Luke 18:22).

This is when the other shoe drops. We learn more information about the identity of this ruler. When he hears Christ's demand he becomes very sad. Why? Because he was extremely rich.

So is Jesus here actually teaching a kind of works righteousness? Is there actually something we can do that would be enough to earn eternal life? Well, in one sense, yes. If you or anyone else kept God's law perfectly, then you would have no need for Christ. You would have a righteousness all your own and salvation would be yours. Of course, if you have ever tried to keep God's law perfectly, you know that in less time than it takes to read this sentence, you have utterly failed. No one, except Christ, has ever kept God's law perfectly, and no one ever will. Jesus was teaching this specific ruler the exact opposite of works righteousness, and he does it by going for the jugular, as it were. The rich man self-righteously claimed that he had kept God's commandments from his youth. Jesus does not get into an argument with him by saying, "Really?" and producing a litany of the man's past sins. Instead Jesus puts the crosshairs on the true affections of his heart. In his case, it was his great wealth. If you want to earn eternal life by your works, then it is simple: your works and the motivations behind them only need to be perfect. All the time. Easy, right?

This is a perfect example of Jesus interacting with a specific man who would justify himself by his works. This is not an overarching teaching that we apply to everyone. Certainly wealth is a stumbling block when it comes to entry into the kingdom of heaven (cf. Luke 18:24; 1 Timothy 6:10). But it is not the only one. If Jesus were speaking to a girl who idolized fame and popularity, perhaps he would have commanded her to delete her Facebook and Instagram accounts, to throw her iPhone in the trash along with all of her makeup and fashionable clothes, and to come follow him. If Christ had been dealing with someone for whom gluttony was a vice, perhaps he would have told him to empty his fridge, give his abundance of food to the impoverished, and come follow him. If it had been the artist who made a god out of her abilities and art, perhaps Jesus would have said to put that all behind her and follow him.

Every single person's heart has affections that they value more than Christ and his eternal gifts. He comes to expose those things in us, not to show us how we can earn his salvation, but to show us how utterly incapable we are of doing so. He comes to show us that even when we do not treasure him and his gifts, he still treasures us, even to the point of death. And that brings us to the second text in question: the parables of the treasure and the pearl.

Most commentators agree that, whatever these two brief parables mean, they are saying the same thing. The most popular application of the parables is this: God's kingdom is valuable. When you find it, give everything you have, and it will be yours. It seems simple and straightforward.

However, if we are consistent with this interpretation, then we have to say that the converse is also true: if we *don't* give everything for the kingdom—whatever that means— then it is not ours. After all, the only reason the treasure or the pearl became the possession of the men is that they first went and sold everything. If they hadn't, the treasure would have remained buried in the field and the pearl would have remained up for sale. Are Christ's gifts of salvation available only to those who give everything for them? If so, what does it mean to "give everything"? And how can I know when I have finally arrived and given my all? Perhaps there is a better, more

Christ-centered, less despairing and less prideful way to interpret these parables.

The key lies in the phrase "the kingdom of heaven." The next time you read the Gospels, especially Matthew, whenever you come across the phrase "the kingdom of heaven/God," think to yourself, *God is up to something here.* That phrase should evoke images of an active reign and rule in which Christ is the king. Christ is the one doing the action. Christ is the subject of the verbs. Christ is up to something.

So, in the parables of the treasure and the pearl, rather than seeing the man and merchant in the parables as stand-ins for ourselves, what if they are actually stand-ins for Christ? When we read it this way, all of a sudden these parables are rich with gospel promises and they make complete sense with the rest of Scripture.

You and I are the treasure hidden in the field and the pearl of great value. Our value is not inherent, but rather comes from Christ's willingness to give everything to have us as his own. And that is precisely what Christ did. He "emptied himself, by taking the form of a servant" (Philippians 2:7). He literally gave all that he had—including his very life—in order to make us children of God. That proclamation kicks us off the pride-despair pendulum and instead assures us that citizenship in God's rule and reign is given to us freely in Christ, without any merit or worthiness in us.

Consider the Comfort

One of my favorite pieces of art hangs above the mantel in my home. In it the artist, Edward Riojas, depicts the risen

Christ. He is in a cemetery, dressed in white with the nail marks in his hands. He has approached one of the graves and, having bent over and thrust his hands into the ground, heaves a full-size casket effortlessly out of the earth.

While the image is rich and stands on its own as a piece worthy of meditation, the artist has also printed words on a scroll that creates the bottom border of the piece. The words take an already beautiful piece of art and infuse it with a gospel interpretation that practically sings. The words read, "For joy, he went and sold all that he had and bought that field."

What a glorious depiction of what our Lord does to have us as his own. He has given his life, entered the grave, and risen again still bearing the marks of his sacrifice. He does it all, and not for glitzy and glamorous jewels. Not for polished people who have their act together and have proven themselves worthy to be treasured. Jesus gives all he has for corpses; people that are dead in their trespasses and sins—people such as you and me. He purchases us precisely so that he can heave us out of our deadly malady and give us everlasting life. The currency he uses is his very own blood. He has died to make you an heir to an eternal inheritance. He has shed his blood in order to present you to himself as a priceless treasure, without spot, wrinkle, or blemish (Ephesians 5:27).

Have you given everything to have Jesus? No, you haven't. But he has given everything to have you. A thing is worth only what someone is willing to pay for it, and Christ paid for you with his very own blood, so that now even you are his treasured possession.

Chapter 3

God Will Help You Accomplish Your Dreams

With God all things are possible.

MATTHEW 19:26

Consider the Claim

It is the basis for countless presentations by Christian or spiritual motivational speakers. They ascend the stage in front of audiences who have come to be inspired, audiences who are struggling to make their dreams a reality. Some people are trying to lose weight. Others are striving to dig themselves out of debt. Some seek marital advice or tips on how to attain that next promotion at work. Parents of unruly children long for methods that will guarantee obedience from their progeny.

And so the expert stands before the crowd, PowerPoint queued and a smile on his face. And one of the first things out of his mouth is, "Just remember. Jesus reminds us that with God, all things are possible."

It is intended to give hope. It is meant to engender motivation and hard work. It holds out the promise that if you strive for your goals and aspire to your dreams, you can do anything you set your mind to, so long as you keep God firmly buckled in as your copilot.

Or perhaps it's spoken by a well-meaning chaplain at a hospital who is ministering to the family of an unconscious young man who has suffered a brain injury. The prognosis is grim. The future is anything but bright. Only a miracle will save him. "Well," says the chaplain, "we take comfort in the fact that with God, all things are possible. Let's pray and hope for a miracle."

Or maybe it's a cry of praise and thanksgiving, like when Motel finally receives Tevye's blessing to marry Tzeitel in *Fiddler on the Roof.* "Wonder of wonders! Miracle of miracles!" With God all things are possible.

Even though it is currently often spoken in a variety of contexts, this single sentence is originally spoken by Jesus in a very specific context. However, as disappointing as it is for our ego, that context has nothing to do with our dreams, passions, or aspirations. But it has everything to do with our salvation.

Consider the Context

In the previous chapter, we witnessed Jesus exposing the spiritual blindness of a man who would seek to justify himself before God by his works. "Good Teacher, what must I do to inherit eternal life?" Jesus, through the interchange he has with the man, teaches that it is quite difficult for a rich man to enter the kingdom of heaven. In fact, it is easier to stuff a six-foot beast of burden through the minuscule eye of a needle than it is for a rich man to enter heaven. If you keep reading, you get to see the disciples' response—which would probably be the response of us all. Amazed at this difficult teaching, they ask, "Then who can be saved?"

This question must set the context for us when we read Christ's reply. To use grammatical terminology, this question concerning salvation is the antecedent to which Christ refers when he says, "With man *this* is impossible" (Matthew 19:26). Salvation, according to Jesus, is impossible for humans to acquire by their works.

The first thing the context ought to show us is that Jesus, in this text, is not concerned about your dreams and aspirations. Jesus is not interested in being your copilot as you pursue your passions. He is not there, cheering you on as you climb the corporate ladder, soaring to success. And, at the risk of sounding insensitive, Jesus in this text is not even interested in granting you the miracle of healing or relief from your intense suffering. No, in this text, Jesus is concerned about one thing: your salvation. That is what the entire exchange between him and the rich man was about, and it is the subject of his disciples' question. Christ's clear answer is that, with man leading the charge, such salvation is utterly impossible.

But he does not stop there. In the way that he frames this teaching, Jesus remarkably places your salvation at the top of his priority list. It is the reason for which he has come. "With man this is impossible, but with God all things are possible." It is a way of saying, "Nothing is too great for God to accomplish.

So great is his power that he is able to accomplish the impossible—even by saving you!" Saving you and all of creation from sin, death, and the devil is the pinnacle of Christ's mission.

Usually we have it reversed in our sinful way of thinking. Usually we think of our entry into God's kingdom—our salvation—as just the beginning point, the thing that gets us started down the path of success. Then we move on to the next steps—the real work of changing the world by realizing our (God-given?) dreams or living the abundant life that God has in store for us (see chapter 18 for more on that). Of course, we never want to leave God behind. That would be foolish. We need him, after all, if we are going to accomplish our dreams. Only when God is with us is everything possible for us.

But in God's kingdom everything is different. Your salvation is the goal, not simply the starting point. It is the thing that is impossible for us, but it is also the very reason for which Christ has come. When we understand that Jesus is not the chair of the booster club that supports our great ideas, when we realize that Jesus is not a side character in our amazing story but that we are in fact made a part of *his* story by grace, then Christ's words in Matthew 19:26 are wonderful gospel. What is impossible for you is a pure joy for Christ (cf. Hebrews 12:1-2). Christ has performed the humanly impossible feat of saving you from death and hell through his death and resurrection for all of your sin.

Consider the Comfort

A parishioner once sent me a link to a video online along with a note indicating he was quite touched by this video: "Isn't this just so inspirational!? Enjoy!" When I clicked on the link, the predictable inspirational music began, and I was greeted by a man with no arms or legs. The video was an incredible account of his story, and the singular theme was simple. Life had been hard for him, full of challenges and setbacks. But none of that got him down. He rose to meet the challenges and has found new ways of operating in this world, because he wanted to make a difference. And here is the key: Jesus has enabled him to do it all. He had found success and he attributed it to Christ's words in Matthew 19:26, "With God all things are possible." (He also threw in a dose of Philippians 4:13 for good measure. See chapter 13 for that one.)

On the one hand, I suppose it was inspirational to see that this man, with God's help, had seemingly overcome every challenge that had been thrown his way. I obviously don't fault him for striving to overcome the challenges that he faces, and I can't even pretend to understand what those must be like. Even so, his use of Scripture was unhelpful at best and despairing at worst. Sure, *he* apparently could do whatever he set his mind to with God's help. God seemed to be on his team, cheering him on and supporting him in all of his endeavors. But what about those for whom the opposite is the case?

That question became quite obvious to me that same afternoon when I was greeted by another person with a lifetime of incredible setbacks. She had arms. But they moved clumsily and with great effort. She had legs. But they were useless stumps, whose growth had been stunted. Her name was Tabitha. She was in her sixties, but had been born with spina bifida. Her whole life she was confined to a wheelchair. I am not saying that Tabitha's life was only misery and hardship. In fact, she had one of the most inspirational stories of anyone. She and her late husband, Martin, were legends around town. He, too, was confined to a wheelchair. And yet, with the help of the community and lots of hard work on their part, they were able to live largely independent lives for decades, zooming all over town in their electric chairs, complete with custom rain covers for the drizzly days.

But the most inspirational part about Tabitha's life was not all that she had accomplished. She never would have made a YouTube video to inspire people with moving motivational nuggets of wisdom that she had acquired in her life. In fact, her language tended to be rather salty and cynical, with a twinkle in her eye that made you know she said it all with joy and love. No, the amazing thing about Tabitha was how she gave witness to Christ. She knew that with God all things are possible. But that statement was not about her. It was about Christ's death and resurrection for her, a sinner, in need of salvation.

It was quite a contrast. On the one hand was the man with no limbs who used his unique weakness to show the world that you, too, can do anything with God's help—the man who treated Jesus as a pick-me-up enhancement drug that allowed him to do all the great things he had accomplished. And on the other hand was Tabitha, who had no dreams of changing the world or any hopes that Jesus would strike her with a miracle to take away her ailment. She was not on a crusade to make her situation worthwhile by using it to transform the lives of those she met. Jesus was not the sidekick to her great and amazing life. Rather, she gave witness to the incredible love and immeasurable power of God: that he had saved even her, and done so in Christ alone. That simple witness affected far more people than she probably ever knew. And that's okay. Because the gospel is about what God is doing in Jesus to save us, even despite us.

Chapter 4

You're a Pretty Big Deal Around Here

I know the plans I have for you, declares the LORD, *plans for welfare and not for evil, to give you a future and a hope.*

JEREMIAH 29:11

Consider the Claim

It was year three out of four in my seminary studies. Typically in our denomination, this is the year that men preparing for ordination are sent on a one-year internship to gain some practical parish experience under the guidance of a supervising pastor. My wife and I had the opportunity to work with the congregation's youth that year, ranging from elementary school to high school.

I will never forget one discussion I had with one of the girls in the youth group. Let's call her Jenny. Jenny was a senior in high school while we were there. She was a straight-A student with conviction and a clear idea of what she wanted to do. That is why I was somewhat surprised when she came to my office one day with a concern: Jenny did not know where she should go to college.

This was strange to me. She had the kind of personality that made me assume she had known where she would go to college ever since elementary school. But I listened to her concerns and the reasoning behind them, and as the discussion moved along, I discovered that one little word had paralyzed her with indecision. It was the word *should*. She did not know where she *should* go to college.

The reason this single word was fraught with crippling uncertainty was that Jenny had been taught the very popular idea that God had a unique, specific, individually tailored plan for her. He had her life meticulously planned out. He had ordained a purpose for her existence from the beginning of time. He knew every detail of her past, present, and future. There was just one little problem: God had yet to let her in on any of it, and she was feeling the angst that is unavoidable when reality collides with such appealing yet false promises. She herself even quoted Jeremiah 29:11 a few times in our conversation, almost as if to convince herself that the angst she was feeling would prove to be worth it in the end. But out of fear of deviating from God's plan for her life, she simply could not decide where she should attend college—that is to say, where *God* wanted her to attend. Jenny was literally afraid to disappoint her heavenly Father.

Jenny's story is not at all isolated. It has become assumed in much modern Christian teaching that God has a unique plan for every individual on the planet. He has the perfect job picked out for you. He has that single person out of seven billion just waiting to be your spouse. He knows every single interaction you are going to have with friends, family, neighbors, and strangers—what you are going to say and how it is going to shape the course of their lives and yours. It is just your job to figure it all out.

I can certainly understand why people believe this teaching. At first blush it is incredibly exciting: to think that God would craft a plan that is unique only to me and no one else and that through my actions I can actually change lives and possibly even the world (all with God's help, of course). I might even start to think that I am a pretty big deal, that I play a necessary and critical role in God's grand scheme for the world, and that if it weren't for me, God might not be able to accomplish his plans. Not to mention, Scripture seems to back up the whole enterprise. "For I know the plans I have for you, declares the LORD, plans for welfare and not for evil, to give you a future and a hope." However, let's look at the context here and truly grasp what this text is saying.

Consider the Context

In the Old Testament history of God's chosen people, we see a pattern emerge. After Adam and Eve fall into sin, God goes about his plan of redemption and restoration. To do this, he gives the promise of a Savior (Genesis 3:15) and chooses a people for himself through whom this Savior would come in order to bear the sin of the entire world. He chooses this people, not because of their righteousness or goodness, but out of his mercy and for the sake of his cosmic plan of salvation. He makes a covenant with them and outlines the consequences: blessings accompany keeping it and failure to keep it brings curses. If you have read the life of Old Testament Israel, then you know that they fail to keep God's commands far more than they succeed.

When God's people Israel rebel against him and chase after other nations and their false gods, there is punishment, which often takes the form of a foreign nation occupying their territory and repressing them. In the context of Jeremiah, that nation is Babylon. By this point in history Israel had been divided into the northern kingdom and the southern kingdom. The northern kingdom had already been dissolved by the Assyrians in the eighth century BC. The southern kingdom had lasted a bit longer, but their disobedience eventually earned them a new home in Babylon, who hauled them off into exile at the beginning of the sixth century BC.

The news of God's judgment did not come unexpectedly. God would send prophets into the midst of his people in order to deliver his word to them. The job of prophet was not a pleasant one. It often meant bringing an extremely unpopular message to people who would rather not hear it. It is no wonder that God's true prophets would often have to contend with false ones. People were far happier to hear the word of a liar, so long as the lie they heard was full of temporal good and well-being. The problem has never really gone away (2 Timothy 4:1-5).

This is exactly the situation we encounter when we read the broader context of Jeremiah 29:11. The genre of this text is simply historical narrative. We are eavesdropping on history that happened over 2500 years ago. For the full story, we need to go all the way back to chapter 27, where we learn basically two things. First, God has appointed King Nebuchadnezzar and his nation of Babylon to be his tool of judgment against Israel (27:6). Second, there will be prophets who will lie through their teeth saying that this is not the case (27:9-11,16-17). They will proclaim that all is well, that there is nothing to worry about, that life will be just fine. In the very next chapter we meet one such prophet.

A man named Hananiah comes along bearing a sweet message for the people of God, claiming to know God's plan for exiled Israel. The only problem is that he did not receive the message from God. Hananiah says that God has broken the yoke imposed by the king of Babylon (28:2) and that within two short years everything will be back to normal for the people of God (28:3,11). Fascinatingly, Jeremiah proclaims that he hopes Hananiah's word comes true, even as he reminds the people that the proof of a true, godly messenger is in the prophetic pudding, as it were: only the prophet whose word comes to pass is to be trusted (28:6-9). After Hananiah finishes preaching his happy lies, God reveals to Jeremiah that Hananiah is indeed counseling "rebellion against the LORD" (28:16). He crafted false promises and winsomely led people astray. So, Jeremiah proved himself to be a true prophet in a sobering way: he prophesied that Hananiah would drop dead within the year. And, in fact, he did (28:16-17). It was never a good idea to contend with God's true prophets; they always won (cf. 1 Kings 18:20-46).

Do you see what is going on here? God is juxtaposing himself and his eternal plans with the trite temporal plans of the false prophets. The false prophets may have a word full of instant gratification that scratches the itching ears of those who hear, but their word will always lead to death (cf. Jeremiah 27:16-17). Conversely, God's true prophets, while bringing a hard word, ultimately bring a word that gives life. That is where we get to our famously misquoted text.

One of God's most amazing attributes is that he does not deal with us as our sins deserve (Psalm 103:10). To be sure, Israel's Babylonian exile was a sign of God's judgment, but it is never judgment without hope, and not the temporal hope that Hananiah proclaims and to which it is so tempting for us to cling. No, God is in the business of giving his people, sinful though we are, true hope and promise, even in the midst of judgment. We see this very thing in Jeremiah 29.

The very first verse of the chapter explicitly informs us of the genre of the next 23 verses, and therefore how we ought to read those verses, especially verse 11. The genre is a letter written by Jeremiah, and we are told that it is addressed "to the surviving elders of the exiles, and to the priests, the prophets, and all the people, whom Nebuchadnezzar had taken into exile from Jerusalem to Babylon." It is pretty simple: if you are a surviving elder of the exiles, a priest, a prophet, or a person Nebuchadnezzar had taken into exile from Jerusalem to Babylon in the sixth century BC, then this letter is written to you (and you are worthy of medical research for having evaded death for the last 2600 years). However, if you are not one of those people—and you are not—then you are simply privileged to eavesdrop on what Jeremiah writes.

The letter goes on to talk about how the exiles should make themselves at home in Babylon. They should establish themselves on Babylonian real estate and eat the food of the land

(29:5); they should maintain the institution of marriage and bear children (29:6); remarkably, they are to maintain a good rapport with the local residents and pray for the city's welfare (29:7). How can God say this to his exiled people? Because he has bigger plans that they cannot yet see. After seventy years their exile will be over, and he will bring them back into the promised land, where they will seek him and call upon him in worship (29:10-14).

There is more to the letter. For example, we could spend a whole chapter on verses 8-9, where Jeremiah warns God's people to beware of those who would claim God spoke to them in a dream or vision (see my chapter 16 to explore that more), but here is the point: Jeremiah 29:11 was not written to you or to me. You and I were never exiled in Babylon for seventy years in the sixth century BC. This is part of a letter written at a specific time, addressing specific events, involving specific people. The promises God gives in this letter are fulfilled in history just as he said: after seventy years, Cyrus of Persia comes to power and allows the exiles to return. They start to trickle back, and under the leadership of Ezra and Nehemiah, the temple is rebuilt and sacrifices resume at the altar of God.

Consider the Comfort

So does this mean that we have nothing to learn from Jeremiah 29:11? In fact, we can learn much. We learn that it is possible to be deceived by a tempting and sweet message, and that God's Word alone is enough to deliver his promises. We learn that those promises are unwavering, and that he will always make good on his Word. In short, we see yet another example of God's faithfulness for his faithless people who do not deserve his mercy. He will not let even human sin disrupt his plan to redeem all of creation in Christ. Even when it appears that all hope is lost, his plan for a Savior continues, woven into history like a precious golden thread.

This is important to bear in mind. For even when the seventy years in Babylon come to completion and God's people begin to return to their homes, it is never as good as it used to be, and it frankly does not last long. Eventually God's people are dispersed, the prophets go silent, and for four hundred years it appears that God may have forgotten the Savior he promised to Adam and Eve so long before. But of course he didn't. As Paul reminds us, "But when the fullness of time had come, God sent forth his Son, born of woman, born under the law, to redeem those who were under the law" (Galatians 4:4-5). With the coming of the Messiah, all the promises of God are now fulfilled, and we have been given God's final revelation of his plan and purpose, not just for his sixth-century people but for all people, of all times and places. We need nothing more, for "long ago, at many times and in many ways, God spoke to our fathers by the prophets, but in these last days he has spoken to us by his Son" (Hebrews 1:1-2).

So how does this help us give an answer to Jenny, who was fraught with fear of deviating from God's mysterious plan and purpose in her college decision? Ironically, the answer that would frequently be given to her would be to ignore the advice of Jeremiah in 29:8-9. So much spiritual "wisdom" would tell us that to discern God's will we should listen to our insides and equate them with God speaking to us: the feelings or intuitions we have, the passions that consume our thoughts, or the "word" we receive from God in deep prayer and meditation or from a fellow Christian who claims to have "a word from God" for us. All of these lead to one of two places: idolatry or uncertain despair. On the one hand, to trust any or all of these things is to functionally deny that God's revealed Word is sufficient. We idolatrously think we need something more. The other end of the pendulum swing, though, is uncertain despair. That is to say, how can I be sure that any of these things is actually God's revelation to me?

Fortunately, there is a better way. I will admit, this alternative way is certainly not as exciting as the prospect that God has a uniquely crafted purpose for my life unlike anyone else on earth. But to rejoice in God's revealed Word alone, not speculating over what he may or may not be up to, is to exchange instant gratification and temporal excitement for true comfort and liberation from uncertainty.

Jenny was not very happy with my answer at first. After listening to her concerns, I simply reminded her that this was not a decision with a right or wrong answer. This was not a decision where she would either make God happy or sad. This was a decision that she got to make in Christian freedom. So rather than encouraging her to speculate about God's will in the matter, I instead encouraged her to consider the practical concerns: Which college was the best bang for her buck? Was living close to home a priority? If so, which one was closer to home? Which college offered the best program of study in which she was interested?

I assured her that in all of it, regardless of the decision she made, God's will for her was still firm, certain, and comforting:

she is God's baptized, died-for-by-Christ child, and that is enough. Jenny did eventually choose a college, loved it, and as far as I know, is joyfully serving Christ's people as a professional church worker.

No matter what your vocation may be, God's will for you is certain and comforting. If you have a husband or wife, then God's will is that you be a faithful husband or wife who rejoices in Christ's gifts. If you have children, then God's will is that you be a faithful parent who rejoices in Christ's gifts. If you have a job, then God's will is that you be a diligent worker who rejoices in Christ's gifts.

When we place our hope in "the plans and purposes of God" that he has not actually revealed to us, we end up placing our hope in something uncertain and self-made. Whether it is our gut feelings and intuitions, or the circumstances of our life that we piece together as some sort of meaningful puzzle to figure out God's will, all of it is, at the end of the day, meaning that we have made up for ourselves.

No, God does indeed have certain, knowable plans for you. His purpose for you is clearly revealed in the Bible, and it is the same for all people: that you would hear and believe in Christ whom he has sent to forgive you all of your sin.

" Chapter 5 "

Dying Is Just a Part of Life

Precious in the sight of the LORD *is the death of his saints.*

PSALM 116:15

Consider the Claim

I had arrived at the hospital only minutes after Gary had died. He was a long-time, beloved member of the church. His wife had died only a few months before, so I had become acquainted with the extended family and was glad to be able to minister to them. When I entered the room, there was nothing but silence. It was that strange moment immediately following death where waves of emotion are washing over the friends and family of the deceased. Obviously there is grief over losing this loved one. If there has been much suffering through the dying process, there is also relief. If the deceased was being cared for by one of their adult children, there can often be a sense of purposelessness now that they are gone. Those moments immediately following a death are great privileges for the pastor, for death has an ironic way of bringing a sobering perspective to life. It is a time when people are grasping for comfort and for answers.

I stood at the foot of the bed, looking at this man to whom I had given pastoral care for the last few years. I silently reflected upon caring for this precious lamb of Christ and thanked God that he had sustained him in the faith even to the end. I remembered the times I visited him and his wife in their home, bringing the gifts of Word and Sacrament into situations that were very challenging for them both. I remembered their stories about how they met and how one of their favorite pastimes was square dancing. I got to hear the stories about raising their children, and I subsequently received the inevitable advice that young pastors receive from older parishioners about childrearing. I got to witness a husband's love as he cared for his wife in her declining health, even though his own health was not very good. I had been given the privilege to hear them laugh and cry; despair and rejoice. And now they were both dead. Even pastors mourn.

"You're probably used to this by now."

The silence created by death had been broken. It caught me off guard.

"Pardon?"

It was Gary's son. He didn't look at me but kept his gaze upon his father. "You're probably used to this by now," he repeated.

"What do you mean?" I asked.

"I mean people dying. You do this all the time, being around when people have died, and it probably doesn't bother you too much anymore, huh?"

I honestly had never even considered such a thing. I shook

my head and told him, "No. In fact, the minute death stops bothering me, that will be the sign that I probably shouldn't be a pastor anymore."

His question reflected a larger perspective that has taken root even in the church. It seems that Forrest Gump's mother has informed more people about the meaning of life and death than any biblical text has. On her deathbed, with light streaming in the windows and everything in its peaceful place (death is hardly ever so serene), she says in a weak but confident voice, "Dying is just a part of life." It's her way of saying what Gary's son had said: we ought to just get used to death.

But the Christian is not so quick to take such a perspective. To say that death is a part of life is a theologically profound thing to say. After all, when we speak about death and life, we inevitably make a confession also about sin, its consequences, and God's answer to it all in the person and work of Christ.

Consider the Context

Whenever we speak about life and death biblically, we must go all the way back to the beginning. There we learn what life truly is within God's design.

In Genesis 1 we are given the account of God creating the heavens and the earth. With systematic order and loving intention he creates all that exists, and he does it with his powerful Word. The refrain repeats over and over: Let there be, and there was. When it is finished, God looks at all that he has created and "behold, it was very good" (Genesis 1:31).

On the sixth day of creation we get to observe God, the heavenly Potter, fashioning the dust of the earth into his most beloved creation: mankind. One can almost imagine the God of the universe stooping down, pushing and manipulating the dirt into the form of a man until his body was just right.

But the man was not yet finished. He was incomplete. Only when God breathed into his nostrils the very breath of life did that lifeless corpse become a fully living human being. God's perfect intention for his human creatures is that they would be fully alive, body and soul integrated as a single person. Death—the separation of body and soul—was not part of the picture that day. Death—the undoing of our very humanity—was indeed *not* a part of life.

Of course, all of that changes in Genesis 3. The deceiver does his work to cast doubt in the good and perfect will of God (3:1-5). Adam and Eve disobey God's Word (3:6), and with that sin, all of creation is cast headlong into decay, shame, suffering, and—you guessed it—death. Now the blessed gift of procreating children would be painful and the relationship between husband and wife would be strained and disordered (3:16). Now the joyous vocation of tending the garden and enjoying its fruit would be laborious, tedious, and thorny work (3:17-18). Now the dust that had been fashioned and breathed into by God to be a fully living creature forever would return to the dust from whence he came (3:19).

Here is the point: death is bad. It is the result of sin. It is a violation of God's created order. It is something that makes us less than the fully human creatures God intends. That may seem obvious to say, but these days the worst we seem to be able to say about death is that it is an unfortunate but unavoidable thing. On the flip side, some even strive to describe death as good or beautiful, the end of suffering or the wonderful gateway into eternal life.

While we can probably find small kernels of truth in such sentiments, the Christian has something less vague and more robust to confess. The Christian ought to confess boldly that death is not part of God's good creation. It is a violation of his perfect order. It is a result of and curse upon sin and disobedience (Romans 6:23). Every time a person draws their last breath, it is a reminder to us that sin and sin's curse still hold sway over us as human creatures. To say that a person has died is perhaps one of the most profound things we can say about them. If we get used to death so that it no longer bothers us and we simply consider it a part of life, then we have forgotten the seriousness of our sin and the consequence it deserves.

But the Christian has even more to say. Not only do we confess that death is not our friend—that it is our great and terrible enemy and the consequence of sin—we also confess that it is an enemy that has been defeated by Christ, the lamb of God who takes away the sin of the world. The wages of sin is certainly death, "but the free gift of God is eternal life in Christ Jesus our Lord" (Romans 6:23). In Adam all people certainly die, but "in Christ shall all be made alive" (1 Corinthians 15:22). The life spoken of in these verses is not a vague, foggy idea of disembodied spirits hanging out in the clouds. Far from it! Over and over again the final and ultimate hope given to us in God's Word is not to die and go to be with Jesus in a vague place we call heaven. The ultimate hope for the Christian is to actually, really, physically live. Our hope is the resurrection of the dead, the undoing of death itself. That is why the psalmist can say in hope, "Precious in the sight of the LORD is the death of his saints" (Psalm 116:15). It is not because death is good in itself. Rather, it is because death, for the saints of God, is temporary.

Even in Genesis 3, after Adam and Eve fall into sin, God is not content to leave them wallowing in that curse. Even there he is quick to proclaim a promise that what they have done, he will undo. He is speaking to the serpent when he says,

> I will put enmity between you and the woman,
> and between your offspring and her offspring;
> he shall bruise your head,
> and you shall bruise his heel.
> (Genesis 3:15)

God does not look upon his creation's sinful condition and say, "Dying is no big deal. It may be unpleasant, but at least you will get to go to heaven and be with me." No, death is precisely the problem. It is the consequence and proof of sin and separation from God. So if there is to be any life at all, God must undo sin and death. And there at the very beginning he promises the one who would accomplish it: none other than Jesus Christ, who is the resurrection and the life.

It would not happen immediately. God unfolds his plan throughout the meanderings of history, and sometimes that promise seems barely visible as his people continue to forsake him, forget him, and turn away from him. But God is faithful, even when his people are not. Nothing will prevent him from fulfilling his promise. So when the time had finally come, God sent forth his Son to redeem those under the law (Galatians 4:4-5).

Christ came to undo what sin had wrought. Not only does he heal the diseases and suffering and decay that sin has brought into the world. Ultimately he takes the sin of the entire world upon himself, and it kills him. The Resurrection and the Life died. The author of life submitted to death. The only innocent One endured the full brunt of God's wrath so that we would not have to. Sin and death—in a profound mystery—were actually victorious over Christ.

Well, at least for three days. Jesus, of course, did not stay dead, but rose in victory on the third day, never to die again. His resurrection was not a mystical, vague, bodiless sort of resurrection. No, sin and death could not ultimately hold him captive, and he rises physically from the grave (Matthew 28; Mark 16; Luke 24; John 20), appears to many people (1 Corinthians 15:5-8), tells Thomas to touch the wounds in his flesh (John 20:24-29), and eats a piece of broiled fish in front of his disciples (Luke 24:41-43). This is no ghost (Luke 24:39). And here's the beautiful thing: now, in Christ, we see a preview of the true Christian hope.

It is because of Christ's death and resurrection that the apostle Paul can say that death and condemnation spread to all men through sin, but justification and life for all men have been won by one act of righteousness (Romans 5:15-21). It is because of Christ's death and resurrection that Paul can refer to Christ as "the firstfruits of those who have fallen asleep" (1 Corinthians 15:20). That means that Christ's was only the first resurrection of many more to come, namely, the resurrection of all flesh on the last day (1 Corinthians 15:21-24), with eternal life being granted to those with faith in his promises. It is because of

Christ's death and resurrection that Paul can refer to death as an enemy that will finally be destroyed (1 Corinthians 15:26). The tomb of Jesus is—and forever will be—vacant, and the same is true for those who die trusting in his mercy.

Consider the Comfort

When we first understand death as the Bible describes it, the Christian church can actually proclaim true, concrete hope in the face of death. It has become too common these days for the church to implicitly deny the serious nature of death in the rituals and language we employ when death occurs. The occasion of death has ironically become an opportunity to have a "celebration of life." When we plan a memorial service, it is often full of nothing but fond memories, nice sentiments, and a vague hope that the deceased is in heaven forever with Jesus. We act as if the body does not matter anymore, since it was "just a vessel" for the soul (never mind that Jesus cares enough about this body to die for it and raise it from the grave on the last day). Too many funeral sermons fail to even mention the reality that this dead brother or sister will rise in glory on the last day. Instead, pastors are content to speak about this death as the final stop, the closing chapter. "He had a good go of it, and now leaves a legacy for all of us."

All of these are ways that the church unintentionally confesses that death is not bad, that it is just a part of life, that this Christian's life has come to an end. Such sentiments fail to give us any substantial hope precisely because they do not reflect the truth of sin and death.

Sometimes I drive past old cemeteries, and if I have some extra time, I will pull over and take a stroll among the graves. Perhaps that sounds morbid. Perhaps it is. But a person can learn a lot about how people view death simply by reading inscriptions on tombstones. One can learn a lot about where people find hope and comfort when loved ones die.

You will see many headstones with familial connections engraved on them. "Loving mother." "Faithful husband." "Beloved child." The comfort in the face of death is that these people were loved by others.

Some gravestones will be emblazoned with the deceased person's favorite hobbies. Apparently the comfort here is that Jim will be eternally fishing in the heavenly ponds, Susan will be scrapbooking in her mansion of craft supplies, and Bob will be perfecting his golf swing on the perfectly manicured greens at St. Peter's Country Club.

Other tombstones will say, "Forever in our hearts," or "We will always remember you." The hope in the face of death is that this person will not be forgotten. In reality, though, it is a hope that will last only two or three generations at most. After all, how many of us remember ancestors beyond our great grandparents? At best we might know our forebearers' names, but probably nothing about their character, their hobbies, their values, and the like. I wonder why we think subsequent generations will be any different.

Some tombstones will be a bit more specific by naming God or Jesus. A common one is, "In the arms of Jesus." This is not necessarily a wrong thing to say concerning the Christian who has died. The problem is that it is vague and unspecific. What does it mean to be embraced by Christ, and do we have to die before we can experience such a thing?

What I have noticed is that one kind of tombstone is conspicuously missing from most cemeteries I have visited. I have yet to read a tombstone inscription that confesses the return of Christ on the last day and the resurrection of the dead to eternal life. Put another way, I have never seen a tombstone inscription that confesses death as a temporary thing, an enemy that has been defeated and will be undone when Jesus returns. The best reason I can think of for this lack of confession is that we have forgotten not only the truth about sin and death but also the amazing, concrete, and physical hope that our Lord gives us in rising bodily from the grave.

It is not as if it would be difficult to do.

"Judy: Baptized child of God, waiting for Christ to return and raise her from the dead."

"Frank: may he rest in peace and rise in glory."

"Laura is in Christ, and so her death is but a temporary setback."

"Christ is risen, and Bill—baptized into Christ, faithful husband, beloved father, and caring son who loved hunting, fishing, football, Bud Light, and the Fourth of July—will rise too."

You get the point. Such inscriptions certainly do not confess *everything* about sin, death, salvation, and the Christian hope. But as Christians we must think of small ways that we can confess the truth of Christ and the fullness of the biblical witness.

Why don't we confess this robust resurrection hope that we have? Why do we settle for vague ideas of hope that only confuse the Scriptures' teaching? We have something better to confess. Let's confess it joyfully. Christ has died. Christ is risen. Christ will come again. And when he does, death is finally done for. Come quickly, Lord Jesus.

Chapter 6

All You Have to Do Is…

*Behold, I stand at the door and knock. If anyone
hears my voice and opens the door, I will come in
to him and eat with him, and he with me.*

REVELATION 3:20

Consider the Claim

The lights have been dimmed. The band's opening set has done a wonderful job setting the stage with music that has led you into the presence of God. The pastor has delivered a meaningful sermon that has pulled at your heartstrings and shown you how much you need God in your life and promised that if you had God in your life, things would be better. And now the moment has arrived. He stands on the stage and talks about how God has made salvation available to all. How Christ's death has made the forgiveness of your sins possible. How God loves all people and there is no one left out; no one has sinned too much. And then it comes. The climax. The denouement. The decision. The pastor utters six little words that indicate God is now showing up to do business—six little words that may very well set the trajectory of an unassuming congregant's life.

"All you have to do is…"

They seem small, harmless. They seem to make logical sense. They seem to take Jesus seriously when he says, in Revelation 3, that he is knocking at the door and that we should be good hosts and open it. And so the service concludes with the raising of hands, the coming up to the stage, the praying of the sinner's prayer by those who have taken the pastor's advice. All they have to do is open their hearts to Jesus. All they have to do is accept him into their hearts. All they have to do is give their whole existence over to him. Then—and only then—will his blood-bought gifts finally be theirs.

This seems to be the way of things in most of popular American Christianity. No one even seems to give it a second thought. This is the assumption about how God saves people. God makes an offer, and the individual either accepts or rejects it. It is simple and formulaic. "All you have to do is…"

However, make no mistake. These words are deadly, giving a false sense of hope and ignoring a critical biblical teaching concerning mankind's natural condition. These words simultaneously underestimate the depth of our sin and overestimate our ability to do something about it. The result is that any certainty of salvation or comfort in the face of our damning sin is stolen from us.

Perhaps you are wondering, "What's the big deal? Why get on a well-meaning pastor's case just because he is trying to get a few people to believe in Jesus?" These words would not be so deadly if we were talking about programming the DVR at home or baking a batch of grandma's chocolate-chip cookies. In those cases, we welcome the instructions that imply such things are easy and simple. "All you have to do is push this button, then that one, then enter this code, and you're all set to be watching your thirty-seven favorite TV shows at your complete leisure." Easy. Simple. Innocuous.

But when we speak about eternity, salvation, and the forgiveness of sins, our language should not be nearly so flippant, as if such things can be obtained by merely following a seven-step program. No, the situation is far worse than that. If there *is* any program that the Bible gives us to apprehend salvation, it is this: all you have to do is be perfect (Matthew 5:48). That's all. No big deal, right?

In order to understand Revelation 3 properly, we must consider it both within its immediate context and within the broader context of Scripture.

Consider the Context

Revelation 3:20 is most often used to exhort unbelievers to place their trust in Jesus by exercising their will. Jesus so desperately wants to come and dwell within their heart, but he is powerless. Or if he is not powerless, he is at least a gentleman who forces himself on nobody. In either case, it is up to the unbeliever to yield to him, to unlock the door of their heart and open it up to him. Only then will they possess all that Jesus wants to give to them. However, a contextual reading of Revelation 3:20 shows us the multifaceted problems with that understanding.

The overarching problem with the popular reading of the

text is that it ignores what the Scriptures teach concerning the
will of the unconverted person. Theologians have made a helpful distinction between the four stages of mankind's will: 1) the
will of man *before* the fall into sin; 2) the will of man *after* the
fall into sin and *before* conversion; 3) the will of man *after* conversion; and 4) the will of man in the resurrection when Christ
returns in glory.[2] This discussion of Revelation 3:20 is primarily concerned with numbers 2 and 3. Since this verse is so often
used to exhort *unconverted* people to believe, let's consider the
Scriptures' teaching on the will of man after the fall into sin but
before conversion.

Perhaps the clearest text in the discussion of mankind's natural state is Ephesians 2:1-10. Paul is writing to Gentile converts
to the Christian faith. The first chapter of the letter is packed full
of gospel promises. He refers to them as "saints" and says they
are "faithful" (1:1). He praises God for adopting the Ephesian
Christians into the family of God through Christ (1:5) who has
redeemed them and forgiven their sins (1:7). He reminds them
that their faith has been worked in them by the hearing of the
word of truth, in which they are sealed with the promised Holy
Spirit (1:13). For all of this Paul gives thanks for the Ephesians in
their love for all the saints (1:15-16) and prays that they would be
given wisdom, knowledge, and enlightenment (1:17-18).

Then in chapter 2, Paul takes some time to remind them
from whence they came—what they were before the word of
truth had taken hold of them. He says in 2:1-3:

> You were dead in the trespasses and sins in which you
> once walked, following the course of this world, fol-
> lowing the prince of the power of the air, the spirit that

is now at work in the sons of disobedience—among whom we all once lived in the passions of our flesh, carrying out the desires of the body and the mind, and were by nature children of wrath, like the rest of mankind.

There are a few noteworthy statements in those verses. Notice how Paul describes them as formerly "dead" in their trespasses, and how this deadness was evident by the fact that they chased after the "course of this world" as "sons of disobedience." They wanted nothing to do with God or his promises. Quite the contrary, they were running in the opposite direction.

Notice also how Paul moves from speaking about the Ephesians specifically to speaking about all people generally. Paul says that "we all once lived in the passions of our flesh" and that we "were by nature children of wrath, like the rest of mankind." Paul, in no uncertain terms, states that all people—with no exceptions—are by nature children of God's wrath.

These three verses alone should be enough to keep Christians from exhorting unbelievers to exercise their will to make a decision for Jesus. Ephesians 2:1-3 teaches us that not only do unbelievers not *want* to believe in Jesus, but they *can't*. They are dead, says Paul. Asking an unbeliever to make a decision for Jesus is like asking a lifeless body to give itself CPR. It would be like Jesus standing at the tomb of Lazarus and telling the four-day-old corpse, "It is easy. All you have to do is start breathing and get your heart beating again." No, the dead unbeliever needs a powerful word that will accomplish what he cannot. Lazarus needs life given to him from outside, precisely because he does not have it himself.

This is exactly how Paul proclaims the solution to the problem in Ephesians 2:4-10:

> But God, being rich in mercy, because of the great love with which he loved us, even when we were dead in our trespasses, made us alive together with Christ—by grace you have been saved—and raised us up with him and seated us with him in the heavenly places in Christ Jesus, so that in the coming ages he might show the immeasurable riches of his grace in kindness toward us in Christ Jesus. For by grace you have been saved through faith. And this is not your own doing; it is the gift of God, not a result of works, so that no one may boast. For we are his workmanship, created in Christ Jesus for good works, which God prepared beforehand, that we should walk in them.

"But God..." Those two little words are overflowing with the gospel. After reminding them of what they used to be, Paul does not continue by saying, "But when you made a decision for Jesus..." No, we were the ones doing the verbs that led to destruction. But God is the one doing all the verbs that lead to salvation, and he does it all through Christ. Paul says explicitly in verse 8 that none of this is our doing. That is a good thing, because if it *were* our doing, we would steal the glory from God and boast about our salvation as if it were a good work that we had performed. Rather, Paul reminds us that the good works we do perform are only the result of having been saved through Christ. And even those are good works for which we cannot take credit, since God is the one who has prepared them.

There are other places we could look to consider the will of the unconverted person (Matthew 15:18-19; John 1:13; Colossians 2:13). But even if we only take Ephesians 2:1-10 at face value, there is no defensible reason to exhort the unbeliever to make a decision for Jesus. Instead, the word of truth (Ephesians 1:13) that grants faith should simply be proclaimed (cf. Romans 10:13-17). Revelation 3:20 must be read in this broader context, lest we make Scripture fight against itself just to satisfy our human reason.

Even if Scripture did teach that an unconverted person could exercise their will unto salvation, the immediate context of Revelation 3:20 shows us that Jesus there is not even speaking to unconverted people.

Revelation 3:20 is quite near the end of a large chunk of the book that starts back in 2:1, where John is given a message to deliver to seven churches in Asia Minor. Each of these brief messages follows a similar pattern. There is often a commendation from Christ, a word of judgment from Christ, and an exhortation to repent and continue in the faith to the end.

On the one hand, each church is faced with unique temptations, and so Christ's exhortation is unique in each letter. On the other hand, he describes temptations that his church has faced in every time and every place. In any case, the point is this: these words are not written to unbelievers. They are written to people who have *already* been granted faith in Christ through the preaching of the gospel, but who have given in to temptation in one way or another.

This means that when we hear Jesus saying, "Behold, I stand at the door and knock," whatever he *is* saying, he is *not* saying it to unbelievers but to Christians. We know this because in 3:14 he says, "And to the angel of the *church* in Laodicea write…"

The church in Laodicea seems to receive the harshest word from Christ, since he does not commend them for anything, as he does with the other six churches. It appears that they are relying on their worldly prosperity and success and forgetting what their true condition is before God. In verse 17 Jesus says, "For you say, I am rich, I have prospered, and I need nothing, not realizing that you are wretched, pitiable, poor, blind, and naked." He goes on in verse 18, exhorting them not to place their trust in worldly treasures but to treasure his gifts of forgiveness, which cover over their shame and nakedness, and to open their eyes to see the truth, which they had apparently left behind.

Then Jesus makes the famous statement that he is standing at the door knocking to come in. Notice that he never says that this is the door of a person's heart. That detail is usually imported by the preacher. No, the context would most naturally indicate to us that this is the door of his church.

When we consider that, it is a sobering image, really. His church had apparently so forgotten his truth that they had put Jesus on the outside of it, and yet were perfectly comfortable because they were doing pretty well for themselves. Now he is on the outside of his own church, asking to come back in. But even that is a polite way to put it. This is more than a request. This is a stern call to repent, to rejoice in the truth, even when the world would call it foolishness. This is a warning *to the church*—not an invitation to unbelievers—to be faithful to the truth that the Lord has given, not deviating to the right or the left, no matter what the cost. For only then will we have true fellowship with Christ.

Let me be crystal clear. I am not saying that if you had the experience of giving your life to Jesus, accepting Jesus into your heart, or praying the sinner's prayer you are not a Christian. What I am saying is that if you have faith in Christ, it is not because of anything you have done but because of everything that God has done for you in Jesus.

This raises important questions concerning how we, as the church, discuss salvation and our role in it. If my salvation is all because of Christ, then why would I try to find comfort and certainty for my salvation apart from Christ? Why point to the day that I did something to be saved rather than the day that Christ did everything to save me? Why continue to exhort unbelievers to do something to attain salvation rather than simply proclaim what Christ has done, trusting that "faith comes from hearing, and hearing through the word of Christ" (Romans 10:17)?

Consider the Comfort

I had been a pastor for about three years when Richard darkened the door of the church where I was serving. He was there because he was dating a woman who was a member of the congregation. I would eventually have the privilege of officiating at their wedding. I remember the first service he attended. When it was over I was greeting folks as they left the sanctuary. When Richard got to me, he said, "That was a service for peasants." I had no clue what he meant, but he was intrigued enough to want to meet with me that week to talk more. At our meeting I asked him what he meant by his comment, and what he told me next would start a friendship that neither of us knew was coming.

Richard's spiritual background was varied, to put it lightly. He grew up an atheist, leftist, feminist, secular humanist whose hope was in the progress of humankind. In his early thirties, through a variety of events, Richard opened the door of his heart and let Jesus in to reign over his life (he would never describe it that way now). He was involved with all manner of Protestant denominations, ranging from extreme charismatic to run-of-the-mill evangelical. Not too long before we met, he was even involved in a healing cult that convinced him to uproot his life and move across the country. But what all of these churches had in common was that they elevated man at every turn.

The leaders and members of these churches were doing great and good things. They were reforming their lives and living in daily joy. They had successful businesses, healing from disease, healthy marriages, well-behaved kids. They were staying clean and sober and faithful. They had stopped gambling and were no longer ever depressed. All of this was the case because they had at one point accepted Jesus into their hearts and were now living the life that proved they loved him.

Well, at least some of them did. Of course, there were those who did not enjoy such blessings, sanctification, and joy: those who were suffering, sinning, and grieving, who even secretly doubted whether they really loved Jesus at all. Richard was one of them. So what was the encouragement he heard in church? Do more. Pray harder, read the Bible more, have more faith, and be more and more obedient to Jesus. Richard and all the people around him were longing for comfort and certainty of knowing they had finally done enough, and instead what they received from these churches was, "Do more." Jesus made an appearance once in a while but was more often a footnote in the great story of every individual member's life.

A couple of decades of hearing those six deadly words "All you have to do is…" had left Richard despairing. He had tried to do more, and it had not worked. His life was not getting better. He was more and more convinced that he was a failure as a Christian. Things that were not even his fault went wrong. He continued to sin. His overall emotions were discouragement and anger. All the hope in himself—which is what it amounted to—was proven to be utterly worthless. After all, how could he ever know that he had done enough when he obviously had not?

Richard heard very different preaching and teaching in the "peasant" church that I served. The teaching was "peasant" because it was not glamorous or humanly attractive. He did not hear about how Jesus came to make your life better. He did not hear about how great mankind is. He did not hear that we should place our hope in our great accomplishments or feelings. He did not hear that for God to be pleased with him he had to have more faith, pray harder, and be more obedient. He did not hear, "All you have to do is…"

Instead, he heard, "Here is everything that Christ has done for you." Rather than hearing mankind elevated and extolled for its great abilities, Richard heard Christ elevated and extolled for his great mercy upon sinful human beings. Richard told me once that he had been a Christian for decades, and this was the first time he had heard the gospel. It did not require an understanding of Greek or Latin. It did not involve subtle analysis of contrasting historical texts. It did not rely on his education or even his culture. It was a message even an uneducated peasant or child could grasp.

The result was that he now had true comfort and certainty

in God's promises, precisely because those promises did not rest upon him but upon Christ. Now if you were to ask Richard how he knows that he is forgiven and made right before God, he would not say, "Because I have accepted Jesus Christ as my personal Lord and Savior by opening the door of my heart to him." He would not say that his comfort lies in the fact that his life is obviously blessed now or because he feels such comfort in his gut. Rather, he would give a mundane, humdrum, peasant answer. He would make God the subject of the verbs: "Because God is merciful to save me, a sinful human being, by his great mercy through the death and resurrection of Jesus, without any merit or worthiness in me."

Don't Be a Hater

Judge not, that you be not judged.

MATTHEW 7:1

Consider the Claim

Part of a pastor's job is to guide people towards a fully biblical understanding of God, themselves, and the world they inhabit. Sometimes this means challenging the Christian brother or sister when they hold a belief or confession that is contrary to God's revealed Word. It is not easy work. Such confrontations are hardly ever enjoyable, except perhaps in hindsight after they bear good fruit. But Christ says that his Word is truth, and so as Christians we have a duty to urge one another on to rejoice in God's truth and live according to it, even when we would sometimes rather make up our own.

This reality requires judgment. It requires us to listen to another person's confession and to be discerning. Does what they confess comport with the truth of God's Word? If so, it is cause for rejoicing. If not, we ought to lovingly confront our fellow Christian with humility and show them, from God's Word, where their error lies. This is judgment—and it is good.

Not everyone agrees with that. Both inside the church and outside the church, there are people who view judgment as a negative thing. To judge seems unloving. It makes people uncomfortable and so we should avoid it, some would say. The fruit of such a perspective is a community increasingly devoid of virtue and confession of sin. Our sinful flesh loves it when judgment is taboo because that means we can indulge in whatever feels right for us, and no one can tell us otherwise.

And yet, judgment biblically understood is actually a blessed thing. It is not only the way that God does his saving work. It is also a way that brothers and sisters in Christ love one another.

Matthew 7:1 is perhaps the single most authoritative text for those who, ironically enough, hate God's Word. They will not have anyone tell them how to live their life or burden them concerning what is right or wrong, true or false. So when a Christian levels a judgment against a certain action or belief, the person being judged—who does not care what the rest of the Bible might say—all of a sudden considers it authoritative and cries out, "Judge not! Jesus said so!"

While Christians cannot be terribly surprised about such a response coming from outside the church, we ought to be diligent that such a perspective does not take root inside our walls. Christians are often exhorted in the Bible to be discerning and to judge the things that contradict God's Word. The reason for this is that whatever contradicts God's Word leads to eternal destruction. And so, out of love, Christians judge. The real heart of the matter is *how* we go about doing it.

Consider the Context

While "Judge not, that you be not judged" is the most well-known verse in Matthew 7, we would do well to keep reading to see what Jesus is teaching. When we keep reading, we discover that Jesus is not telling us never to judge anything or anyone. Rather, he is teaching us *how* to judge. Rather than judging others and their sin in a self-righteous way, Jesus would have us be discerning and careful in our judgment. Rather than ignoring our own sin or thinking that we are somehow better than the other person, we are to recognize that we are all in the same boat. This is not a justification to overlook sin, but rather a way to love one another as fellow sinners under the mercy of Christ.

To convey this teaching, Jesus uses an image that, upon some reflection, is painfully humorous. He says, "Why do you see the speck that is in your brother's eye, but do not notice the log that is in your own eye? Or how can you say to your brother, 'Let me take the speck out of your eye,' when there is the log in your own eye?" (Matthew 7:3-4).

Imagine meeting the doctor who will be performing precision surgery on your eyes. When he walks into the room, he has a telephone pole sticking out of his head through his eye socket and bumbles around before taking his seat, knocking pictures off the walls and jostling the containers on the counter. Every time he turns his head you have to duck to avoid being clobbered with the log. It sounds like a comedy routine from *The Carol Burnett Show.*

That is what it is like to try to judge the sin of another without recognizing your own condition. And yet, far from a comedy routine, it is dangerous, self-righteous foolishness that will only harm both you and the person you are trying to help.

So what is Christ's exhortation? He certainly *does not* say, "Because you have a log in your own eye, just live and let live. You are all sinners anyway, so don't worry about it. Sin is no big deal, so don't judge. Don't be a hater. It's not polite." No, Jesus says that we are to take the log out of our own eye first. We are to take an honest look at our own sinful condition, confess that we ourselves have fallen short, and be forgiven in Jesus. Why? Precisely so that we *can* judge and do so with humility and clarity.

Consider the Comfort

My wife tells a story that I am sure will become canonical in the annals of Suelzle lore. She and her sister went on a camping trip with their dad to Big Bend National Park in Texas. I have never been to Big Bend National Park, but I hear it takes about two years to travel there at peril of death and starvation. Texas is big, y'all.

One of the days they decided to embark on a substantial hike—fifteen and a half miles around the rim of an entire mountain range that is fully contained in the park boundaries. The hike was as one might expect. Wildlife, flowers, and deadly snakes accompanied them throughout the day, as the blazing sun threatened to burn them alive. But the best part of the story is hearing my wife describe the meal they had at a local restaurant after the long day's hike. You might think it was a five-star establishment with some of the finest chefs in the world. She had a pork chop. But not just any pork chop. It was an amazing, flavorful, perfectly cooked, delightfully seasoned specimen of culinary talent. And the iced tea? Oh, the tea! Bottomless glasses of heavenly nectar. Nothing so refreshing had ever graced her taste buds.

Now, I have never patronized this restaurant, so I do not mean to imply that the food there is not good. However, I am willing to bet that my wife's perspective—her judgment—on the food would have been quite different if she hadn't spent the entire day hiking fifteen and a half miles around the mountains in the blazing heat and fending off venomous serpents.

I recount this story to illustrate something similar in the church. God has placed into our possession the wonderful good news of Christ. Christ has died for our sin, risen for our justification, and sustains us in the faith delivered once for all to the saints. You and I have been saved for one reason alone: Christ has done it all.

That is good news, to be sure. But sometimes we forget just how good that news is because we also forget how badly we need it. When God's condemning law is avoided, when talk of sin is left out for fear of hurting someone's feelings, or when we simply avoid judgment to "live and let live," not only are we failing to recognize our true spiritual condition; we are also robbing one another of the comfort of the gospel. If I am a pretty decent fellow already—sure, I make some mistakes, but I try not to—then the news that Christ has saved me really is not all that powerful. It would be like me eating at the restaurant my wife raved about without having hiked fifteen ("and a half!" shouts my wife) miles before. The food would be good, I'm sure, but nothing like her experience.

However, when our truly parched and famished condition is proclaimed to us in all its fullness, now the gospel becomes the sweetest news we could ever hear (consider the account of Nathan confronting David with his sin in 2 Samuel 12). When we are shown that we are by nature enemies of God, objects of his wrath, and deserving of death and hell, then the good news that we are forgiven in Christ is the only thing we want to hear, and we will cherish it all the more.

Such is the rhythm of life within the body of Christ. We love one another by not settling to let our brothers and sisters stray off into sin. We love one another by judging sin, calling it what it is rather than ignoring it. We judge sin, not so that we can condemn, but rather so that the gospel can be proclaimed all the more wonderfully—so that all of us can repent and rejoice even more in God's judgment upon us in Christ: forgiven.

Chapter 8

Everything Happens for a Reason

We know that for those who love God all things work together for good,
for those who are called according to his purpose.

Romans 8:28

Consider the Claim

One of the most difficult funerals I have ever had to perform was for a man who had killed himself. I received the phone call right before our little parochial school's chapel service one Wednesday. I listened as the new widow cried her pain into the telephone, beside herself with grief. I was just as dumbfounded as she was. Her husband's suicide was a shock to everyone who knew him.

Certain kinds of tragedy elicit unique sorts of grief. When a child or young person is killed suddenly or is diagnosed with a terminal illness, it creates a different kind of mourning than when our ninety-three-year-old grandma dies in her sleep. And another sort of grief hits us like a tidal wave when someone we love takes their own life, and that grief is saturated with the question, "Why?"

That is not to say that such a question is absent from other kinds of suffering. However, the difference is that, unlike the child dying or the young mother getting in a fatal car accident, with suicide there is ultimately no answer to the question and there is nothing to be done about the situation. At least when someone is killed by a drunk driver, we can point at the drunk driver and say, "This happened because you made a really bad choice and now you must suffer the consequences." We may not know why a child is diagnosed with cancer, but at least we have medical professionals that we can point to and say, "Help us fight this with everything we have." We retain at least a modicum of control over the situation.

But with suicide it is different. While we can try to sort through a person's past and psychoanalyze his personality and piece together a reason why, at the end of the day all the answers to that question remain locked up in the mind of the one who took his own life. It is not surprising that friends and loved ones so often fill in the blanks by asking, "What could I have done that might have prevented this?" It is a way of grasping for control; it is ultimately a search to answer the question, "Why?"

Unfortunately, one of the most common answers that well-meaning Christians give in the face of such tragedy is to say that "everything happens for a reason." It is an attempt to give comfort, to help the grieving to look to the future in hope, to promise that somehow what seems senseless now will one day make sense. Give it enough time and prayer and it will eventually become clear what God is up to in this tragedy. These were some of the things in which the family sought to find comfort after their husband, father, brother, uncle, and friend had taken his own life.

For the funeral, the family and I had agreed that one of the sons would read the obituary before the service started. What he chose to do instead, much to my surprise, was offer the congregation some thoughts to consider. "Many of you here today might be wondering the same thing that we have wondered much in the past weeks. You are probably wondering why this happened." And then, looking up from his notes, he firmly and passionately said, "Let me tell you something. We. Don't. Care. Why." The son proceeded to speak about how wonderful and loving his dad was—which, by all accounts, he was. But the passion with which he spoke, the calculated fervency with which he uttered those words—"We. Don't. Care. Why."—betrayed the fact that he cared very much why his dad did this, but he could not find an answer.

And yet he searched long and hard for one. As he continued, he said something that grabbed my attention. He spoke about how, because this thing had happened, as terrible as it was, it had brought family and friends together. It had created an opportunity to remember Dad and his love and how full a life he had lived. Of course, such platitudes are hard-pressed to silence the nagging reality that the reason we had all gathered was precisely because a life had ended in an incredibly horrific way. While he did not say it outright, the son basically told us that "everything happens for a reason," and the reason this happened was to bring us all together. That was it. He had discovered the ounce of control that he could have in the situation. That was the best answer he could muster. That was supposed to be the comfort for all of us gathered there. Our coming together with fond memories was somehow supposed to justify the horrible death of this brother in Christ.

And why shouldn't he say that? After all, "all things work together for good," right? Those words are straight from the Bible, and they are often spoken in situations just like the one I have recounted above. However, Romans 8:28 is a verse that, when spoken in a certain context, actually becomes vapid and trite. It is one of those verses that well-meaning Christians can rattle off as if it fixes everything. Are you suffering? Well, don't worry. "For those who love God, all things work together for good." Everything happens for a reason, right? But releasing those words flippantly into the suffering of another person, without understanding and proclaiming their context, is one of the most unhelpful things a person can do.

Consider the Context

Romans 8 is a chapter that I have found myself gravitating towards as I minister to people in their suffering. I have recited the promises of Romans 8 to parents that had lost their child. I have read it at the bedside of a dying woman, whose labored breathing sounded forth a death rattle so loud that the cadence of my words had to match the rhythm of her breathing just so they could be heard. I have taught Romans 8 to young confirmation students, whose world is so small that they have almost no idea what suffering is.

I have shared these words with Christ's lambs because they are words full of promise and comfort. No matter what sort of suffering has caused me in all of those situations to reach for my Bible and thumb open to Romans 8, I have inevitably learned to cherish these promises even more. Not because this part of Scripture gives us all the answers in the face of suffering, but because it gives us promises that ultimately bring our quest for answers to an end.

In the first three chapters of Romans, Paul makes the case that every single person, Jew and Gentile alike, is accused and condemned under the withering law of God. Then in chapter 3, after painting us into a corner, stopping our mouths, and silencing every excuse that we might think of to justify our sin, Paul proclaims what God has done in Christ. Christ's death is the only way that God can be both just to punish sin and able to justify the sinner. In chapter 4, Paul argues that this gift of salvation and faith is not our own work. In chapter 5, Paul shows how Christ's salvation is the undoing of Adam's fall. Adam brought sin and death into the world, the very things Christ comes to destroy. In chapter 6, Paul gives us this incredible promise that in baptism we are buried and raised with Christ and are given the newness of life in which we walk. We are now slaves to Christ rather than slaves to sin. Then we come to chapter 7.

In chapter 7, Paul describes the life of the baptized. It is not all roses and rainbows. Now that the baptized person has been shown the truth, he can more clearly see not only his sin but also his inability to conquer it. To be baptized, you see, is to fight. It is to wage daily war between the old self and the new. Romans 7 is where Paul famously describes what we all know in our experience: we know the good that we want to do, but we fail to do it. We hate evil, and yet are tempted to its wiles. And notice how Paul ends the chapter: "Wretched man that I am! Who will deliver me from this body of death?" (7:24). His answer is not that he will try harder next time, or stop backsliding into sin, or rededicate his life to Christ for the thirty-seventh time, or get endlessly rebaptized. No, his only hope is Christ (7:25).

All of that gives us the necessary context for chapter 8. When we are encountering the suffering of the baptized life, it is tempting to believe that God has forsaken us in the present. When suffering strikes, Satan comes in with his filthy lies and says, "Do you see what's happening? I thought God loved you! I thought that you are baptized! Isn't life supposed to be going easier for you? Perhaps you are suffering because you are so sinful. Everything happens for a reason, and the reason this is all happening is because God is punishing you. If you were a better Christian, none of this would be happening. You might as well give up."

When the accuser hurls such nasty lies at us, and when the sufferings of this world seem too much to bear, Romans 8 gives us a new, eternal perspective. Starting in verse 18, Paul compares our present sufferings with the future glory that is on its way. He describes this glory as "the revealing of the sons of God" (v. 19) and says that the entire creation is waiting for it with eager longing.

So what exactly is this glory? What is this event that cannot come soon enough for the entire creation? In a word, restoration. The way that Paul describes it is masterful. He paints a picture of the whole creation creaking and groaning under the weight of sin and sin's consequences. Ever since the fall of our first parents in the garden, the entire cosmos has been held in bondage to decay, suffering, and death. But the groaning is not like that of old age. This groaning is not unto death. Rather, it is like the groaning of a woman in labor. It is painful, to be sure. (At least, it appears so. I would never be so chivalrous as to take my wife's place during the labor of any of our four children. I'm a total wimp.) But the labors of childbirth give way to something glorious: new life. When that child is finally held in the cradle of her mother's arms, the pains of labor lose their sharpness, for suffering has given way to life (cf. John 16:21).

All of this is the "good" that will come out of our suffering. It is an eternal good, an everlasting purpose, which is no secret, but is a promise made in Jesus. All of this is why Paul can say that there is nothing that can separate us from the love of God (Romans 8:38-39). It is not because suffering is no big deal, but because he has dealt with our suffering on the cross of Jesus.

So when Paul says that "for those who love God all things work together for good," he is not saying that it is your love for God that determines how your life will unfold. He is not giving reasons why this or that suffering is happening to you or anyone else. He is giving comfort and hope by saying that, ultimately, God will make all of this suffering right again, and he has given a glimpse of that in his Son, Jesus Christ, who is risen from the dead.

Consider the Comfort

Christian apologist Ravi Zacharias has said on more than one occasion that if God were to give us 1000 answers to all the questions we ask to force him to justify himself to us, we would demand 1001. He is right. Any answer God may give us as to why this or that suffering is happening might satisfy us for a time, but every answer inevitably brings more questions. We will find more reasons why the answers are not satisfactory, and we will try to pin God to the wall until he gives us what we demand. Thankfully, he does not satisfy our intellect like that. In his mercy, he protects us from the illusion that we have things under control. Instead of answers, he gives us promises, and those promises are enough.

I stepped into the pulpit on that Saturday morning with trepidation. A man's son had just provided the congregation an answer to the question "Why did this man take his own life?" I was there to speak into a situation for which there were no answers. I had prepared a sermon, but I knew I was going to have to depart from it a bit to address the false comfort that had been provided in the son's eulogy. And so, instead of speaking about things we did not know, instead of speculating about this man's eternal fate, instead of playing the zero-sum game, calculating whether he was a good enough person to outweigh his sin or whether he had time to repent in the nanoseconds before he died, instead of trying to interpret some contrived good that God might be working in this horrible event, instead of any of that, I rested upon the certain truth of God's Word and proclaimed Christ.

I proclaimed that death, no matter how it happens, is always the result of our sinful condition. I proclaimed that no matter how much we want to think otherwise, we all rightly deserve eternal death and damnation. I proclaimed that there is nothing that any of us can do to lift ourselves out of the sludge of our enmity with God. I proclaimed that Christ in his mercy has come into that sinful mire precisely for us, his sinful enemies. I proclaimed that Christ, who knew no sin, has become sin for each and every one of us, enduring the full wrath of God in our stead. And I proclaimed that there is nothing that can separate us from the love of God in Christ. I proclaimed that when Christ returns on the last day to usher in the glory we have been waiting for all this time, all the tears and pain and suffering and loss and even death itself will all be undone, and that in the meantime his promises—not his answers—are enough for us.

I have to admit, none of that satisfies my intellectual longing to have suffering figured out. Those promises do not allow me to plug humanity's terrible suffering into some grand equation that will pop out a nice, clean answer. But those promises do drive me to repent of my sin; they drive me to rest not upon my own righteousness and good works, but upon the mercy of God in Christ alone; they drive me to look for the resurrection of the dead and the life of the world to come.

That man's widow approached me after the funeral and thanked me. Through her tears, she simply thanked me for proclaiming Jesus. The promises of Jesus had done their work. Not even this horrible suffering could separate her from the love of God. God had promised as much in Jesus. And that is the same promise he makes to you. In your suffering, great or small, Jesus will not forsake you as you press on in hope towards the day of his return, when every enemy will finally and forever be put under his feet.

Chapter 9

All You Need Is Love

Love is patient and kind; love does not envy or boast; it is not arrogant or rude. It does not insist on its own way; it is not irritable or resentful; it does not rejoice at wrongdoing, but rejoices with the truth. Love bears all things, believes all things, hopes all things, endures all things.

1 CORINTHIANS 13:4-7

Consider the Claim

We have all been there. Sitting in the pew in the sanctuary—or in the rented lawn chair in front of the outdoor gazebo—gazing at two people who gaze at one another in love. Friends and family have gathered to witness these two promise their lifelong devotion to one another. In sickness and in health, for richer or poorer, better or worse, until death steals one of them from the other.

People love weddings. They are a time of solemn promise and joyous celebration. Christian weddings especially bear witness to the world that this is a good and sacred institution of God that is worth entering into and worth fighting for, since it is a mysterious reflection of Christ and his church. It is an opportunity for those who are already married to be reminded of their own vows to their spouse. It allows our children to see God's holy order of love, marriage, and baby carriage in a world that despises that order at every turn. Weddings are great. Love abounds.

And that is why 1 Corinthians 13 is the go-to wedding text for so many. It extols love above all things, and does so in masterful and beautiful prose. "Love is patient and kind; love does not envy or boast…" It is so pithy and beautiful that we cross-stitch it and hang it in our kitchens. We print it on old barn wood, highlighting the word *love* with swirly, flowing font, and sell it at craft shows. We repost it on our Facebook wall, with a blurry background picture of two young lovers holding hands and leaning on one another's foreheads. People love this text of the Bible, even if they are not Christians. It seems a no-brainer to read and speak about this text at the place where love so obviously abounds: the wedding.

The problem is that 1 Corinthians 13 is not about marriage at all. The wedding is not what Paul had in mind when he penned these incredible words by the inspiration of the Holy Spirit. Paul was not thinking ahead, knowing that people would need some good fodder to consider on their wedding day, so he sat down and wrote this poem of love as another way to help make the bride's day perfect and unforgettable. This text is not given so that we can all get goosebumps when we hear its prose, or so that mothers of the bride have something to weep over. This text applies to husbands and wives only insofar as they are also brother and sister in Christ.

The love that Paul speaks of here is of a different sort than the popular, vague, gushy notions of love in our culture. Paul here is writing as a pastor to the Corinthian church, which was rife with division.

Consider the Context

When you venture to read 1 Corinthians, your journey has barely begun before you learn why Paul wrote the letter. He is responding to correspondence that had been sent to him by Chloe (1:11). The subject of this correspondence was a plethora of division that had arisen in the Corinthian congregation.

A survey of these divisions will almost make you sick to your stomach. The church had split itself up into factions, each with their own leader (1:12). While they consider themselves very wise and spiritual people, Paul cannot even address them as spiritual people but only as infants because they are behaving as people of flesh (3:1). Their life together is fraught with jealousy, strife, arrogance, and boasting (3:3; 4:6-7; 5:6). Sexual immorality that is shameful even to pagans is being tolerated among the Christians (5:1). Brothers in Christ shamefully drag one another to court in front of unbelievers because they are unable to settle their disputes peacefully among themselves (6:1-11). Licentiousness is practiced in the name of gospel freedom (6:12-20). Strong believers despise the consciences of weak believers with regard to the meat that has been sacrificed in the pagan temples (8:1-13). The godly ordering of husbands and wives is apparently being despised (11:1-16). The supper that Christ

instituted and graciously gave to his church as a wonderful gift
is being abused as societal and cultural influences—rather than
being left at the door—are informing how they practice (11:17-
34). Some are claiming that they are super Christians because
they have amazing "spiritual" gifts, and they despise those who
have none, thus stratifying the body of Christ (12:1-31; 14:1-19).
To top it off, some were denying the very resurrection of the
dead, despising one of the most central doctrines of the Christian faith (15:1-58).

While the divisions are many and varied, the thing that they
all have in common is that the Corinthians appear to be justi-
fying themselves by appealing to their supposed "wisdom" and
Christian freedom. They are acting super spiritual, but in fact
are just as fleshly as the world around them. The wisdom they
are following is not what they learned from Christ, and it is tear-
ing them apart as a congregation. They have a lack of love for
one another.

The entire context of 1 Corinthians does not allow us to
pluck chapter 13 out and read it on our sentimental terms. Far
from being a nice feel-good poem about how great love is, it is in
fact an admonition to those who are failing to live as they ought.
Paul is not praising them but chastising them.

To the ones who claim that their unintelligible babbling in
tongues proves that they are real and true Christians, Paul basically says, "Big deal. Even if you spoke the heavenly language
of the angels, it would mean nothing because you are using it
to boost your pride and status." To the ones who think they
are quite wise in their understanding and have very important
things to say that everyone should hear, Paul could have easily

said, "What's your point? Even if you understood every mystery of the universe, it would mean nothing, because you are not using that knowledge to serve your fellow Christians in love." To the ones who think their faith is something to behold, that it is so strong they could move mountains with it, Paul pretty much says, "So what. Without love you are nothing." To the ones who would point to how much they have given up to follow Christ as proof of their devotion to him, Paul might as well say, "You have less than you think you do because your pious poverty is self-serving. Your true poverty is that you do not have love."

Paul, acting as a caring and firm pastor, is exhorting these beloved lambs of Christ to love one another. He wants them to see that every member of the body needs every other member.

Consider the Comfort

Have you ever gotten up in the middle of the night to use the bathroom, and in your stumbling stupor, stubbed your toe on the dresser? It hurts. Even if it is the smallest toe that you have—a member of your body that you probably never even think about—in that moment you cannot think of anything else. Your entire body bends over in pain to attend to this one little member that is hurt.

That is how the body of Christ ought to love one another. When one member hurts—regardless of how small or insignificant they may seem—every member hurts. When one member is struggling, the whole body ought to rush in and attend to their needs. True love among the body of Christ is to operate according to the wisdom of humility given to us by Christ. In

the church, no one is greater than the other. The worldly defini-
tions of strong and weak, success and failure are turned upside
down because humble and selfless love rules the day.

But what about weddings? Notice how, when we under-
stand the context of the Bible's "chapter of love," it actually gives
us concrete ways to talk about love, even at a wedding. While
there are other texts that are perhaps even more appropriate for
weddings (for example, Genesis 2 and Ephesians 5), I certainly
would not say we should avoid using 1 Corinthians 13. However,
perhaps we should change the way we speak about it. We ought
to avoid all this talk about how "your love for one another will
get you through the tough times" because frankly, one of the
tough times the couple will endure is that their loving feelings
for one another inevitably wane.

Instead, we ought to speak the truth to them. That there will
be times when they will not want to live self-sacrificially for one
another. They will compete with each other by keeping score,
each one tallying up their own righteous deeds against the failings of the other. They will look for ways to justify their sin
against one another, living in pride. They will each be tempted
to try to get their friends and family on their side when they are
having a disagreement. In short, their sin will tempt them to
live like the Corinthians—without love.

So they need to be reminded that true love is patient, kind,
not jealous or proud, and all the rest. True love always places the
other before oneself. They need to be reminded that they are
two sinners entering a holy union, and that the thing that will
carry them through is not their faltering love for one another,
but Christ's steadfast love for them both. For, after all, he is the

exemplar of 1 Corinthians 13. He is love incarnate, not in that he had nice, positive feelings for us, but that he willingly gave up his life for his sinful enemies.

So for the husband and wife—and for all brothers and sisters in Christ—repentance and forgiveness win the day. We forgive one another in Christ, just as Christ has forgiven each of us. Self-sacrifice that flows from such forgiveness is the rhythm that guides the life of Christ's church as we serve one another in love.

Chapter 10

Name It and Claim It.
Blab It and Grab It.
Reckon It and Beckon It.

As [a man] thinketh in his heart, so is he.

PROVERBS 23:7 (KJV)

Consider the Claim

Have you ever known someone whose life seems to be constantly in chaos and disorder? Some people have such disorder coming to them. They make consistently poor decisions, alienate their loved ones, burn bridges, and blame all their problems on everyone else. I am not talking about those sorts of folks. I am talking about someone who, for all their effort and good intentions, simply cannot get a handle on things. They truly seem to have been dealt the proverbial bad hand of cards. Gloria was one of those people.

Gloria would call me every couple of weeks to share with me her latest calamity. Gloria was an intelligent woman. She never blamed anyone for the problems she was experiencing. She simply recognized that these things seemed to be her lot in life and she was willing, for the most part, to cope with them.

But Gloria would often say something that I found interesting. After reciting her litany of issues, she would say, "Oh, Pastor. I shouldn't be talking about these things in such negative terms. I need to think positively. I need to speak good words over these situations in order to make them better." For as level-headed and intelligent as she was, it was strange to hear her speak as if she thought her words could magically effect change in her life by the mere uttering of them, either for the better or for the worse.

This is, in fact, how some people understand the workings of the Christian life. It is Tinkerbell theology. Think happy thoughts and you can soar. Some people subscribe to a mild version that simply consists of trying to have a positive outlook on life. However, others—such as those involved in the Word-Faith movement (or Word of Faith movement)—believe themselves to be basically little gods who, by speaking words, can actually change reality itself, creating calamity or advantage for themselves.

The idea is simple. Your words create reality. Therefore, if you want a good and prosperous reality, then you must think and speak good and prosperous words. In addition, you must avoid negative and hindering words because what you speak may actually come to pass. It is basically a theological version of *Saturday Night Live*'s Stuart Smalley, who boosted his self-esteem by looking in the mirror and repeating the mantra, "I'm good enough, I'm smart enough, and doggone it, people like me!" I never really liked Stuart.

While a web of misquoted Bible verses has been used to weave this false teaching, there is one verse that takes the cake. It is usually quoted from the King James Version, it is taken out of context, and only the first half of the verse is usually quoted. The verse is Proverbs 23:7a: "For as [a man] thinketh in his heart, so is he."

With that single verse many Christians of at least two generations have been taught that if they can name it, they can claim it; if they can blab it, they can grab it; if they can reckon it, they can beckon it. Health, wealth, and prosperity are all theirs for the taking, as long as they think and speak the right words. Who knew that Christian hocus-pocus was actually a thing?

Consider the Context

It is fascinating that so-called Bible teachers get away with quoting Proverbs 23:7a as justification for the Word-Faith theology. Simply opening a Bible and reading the verse once or twice in context is enough to refute the claims of the Word-Faith teachers.

First, consider the genre of literature into which the book of Proverbs fits. Proverbs is not historical narrative, like Samuel, Kings, the Gospels, or Acts. It also is not doctrinal in the same way as Paul's letters to the churches. Neither is it prophetic, like Isaiah or Ezekiel.

Instead, Proverbs is called wisdom literature. Other books in this genre include Job, Ecclesiastes, and Song of Songs. Such books, while they may include historical narrative and straightforward doctrinal teaching, are more poetic and filled with nuggets of wisdom.

Proverbs is perhaps the clearest example of wisdom literature in the Bible. As you read through Proverbs, the nuggets of wisdom are sometimes only one verse long. Sometimes you struggle to see how one verse connects to the previous one and the one that follows it. And that's okay. It is how all proverbs work. They are meant to be read and reread to tease out their meaning.

The kind of advice that Proverbs gives shows us how godly wisdom plays out in the world. Some of the wisdom is very practical, and on some levels could be helpful for anyone. For example, "Whoever spares the rod hates his son, but he who loves him is diligent to discipline him" (Proverbs 13:24). That axiom is true whether a person is a faithful Christian or not. Other parts of the wisdom are more "spiritual." For example, "The fear of the LORD is the beginning of wisdom" (Proverbs 9:10).

With that overarching context of the book in mind, consider Proverbs 23:7 specifically in its immediate context. First, the verse begins with the word "for." This means that it is in the middle of a thought. Something has been said previously and now this verse is going to further explain it. Second, the verse contains the pronoun "he." Never once do the Word-Faith teachers go back and talk about who the "he" is. They simply generalize the pronoun as if it refers to all people: "For as *a man* thinketh in his heart, so is he." Unfortunately, that is not quite what the text says.

When we hear this verse quoted all by itself, we should immediately ask at least two questions. First, what is it explaining, since it begins with "for"? Second, who is the "he" in this verse?

To answer those questions is pretty easy. Simply back up a single verse. Here are verses 6 and 7 in their entirety, this time in the ESV:

> Do not eat the bread of a man who is stingy;
> do not desire his delicacies,
> for he is like one who is inwardly calculating.
> "Eat and drink!" he says to you,
> but his heart is not with you.

Apparently Proverbs 23:7 is explaining to us why it is not wise to eat a stingy man's bread. I will admit that this verse is not the clearest one in the Bible. But it seems to be saying that if a stingy man appears to be buttering you up with good food and drink, do not think too much of it. He may seem quite giving, but the whole time he is taking inventory of every bite you take and resenting you for it. His true character is not seen in how generous he seems but rather in his heart. I could be wrong, but that appears to be the gist of it.

Regardless of my interpretation, this verse *certainly* has nothing to say about how to overcome suffering or hardship, as the Word-Faith teachers would have us believe. They attempt to use this verse to bring comfort to the person struggling with low income, poor health, or any number of maladies. Not only does this text give no instruction in such things, but to claim that it does only heaps up more uncertainty and despair upon the one who is already suffering.

The most extreme Word-Faith teachers will claim that it is possible to overcome terminal cancer by simply declaring victory over your disease. They will claim that if you want a specific job or promotion, then you need to wake up every morning and start claiming that job for yourself in the name of Jesus. (I have always been curious why some of these teachers wear glasses. If I had such powers as they claim to have, perfect vision would be one of my first divine declarations.)

But what happens when your cancer does not go away? What happens when someone else gets the new job that you had claimed as your own? And why focus on such insignificant things? Why not go big and declare immortality over your life so that you will never die? Some have indeed tried that very thing. You can probably go visit their graves and see how well it worked.

In a well-intentioned attempt to liberate suffering people from their hardships, the Word-Faith movement only places people in more bondage.

Consider the Comfort

One of my favorite old television shows is *The Twilight Zone* from the 1960s. The short and often cheesy vignettes raise fascinating questions about humanity, morality, ethics, science, and our place within the universe. In episode 73, "The Good Life," we meet a monster that has ravaged a small, peaceful town. But he has not done it with claws and sharp teeth; he has not knocked down buildings with powerful arms or killed any of the inhabitants. Rather, he uses his mind. He simply thinks, and reality changes. If he does not like a truck on the street, he simply thinks it away. If a house is in his way, a mere thought will make it disappear. But his mental reign is not limited to inanimate objects. No, if any of the citizens of that town displease him, he can even think calamity upon them, or worse, think them into nonexistence. This monster is the envy of every Word-Faith teacher.

As a result, everyone is smiling. On the surface of things, the entire population of the town is happy and content. However, the reality is that everyone is afraid to anger the monster. The ultimate goal of life is to remain constantly on his good side, no matter how bad life may be going. If someone asks how you are doing within earshot of the monster, your answer had better be, "Great! Couldn't be better!" By their words they keep themselves from calamity, even though they are miserable.

The Word-Faith movement creates a similar atmosphere. However, the monster is not located outside of you, but rather inside. Those who think their words create their reality are in a constant battle between what they know to be true through their experience of suffering and what they are willing to talk about with their lips. People under such teaching become enslaved to the positive. No longer are they able to speak truth concerning the bad things that are going on in their life for fear that they might perpetuate such things even more. Instead, they are told to buck up. Do not anger the monster. Look in the mirror and speak happy, positive, life-changing words over yourself. As Robert Schuller quipped in his final sermon at the Crystal Cathedral, "The me I see is the me I will be." Such teaching puts people in a despairing prison of optimism.

Scripture, thankfully, gives us a better way, a more comforting and certain way. Christ comes and sets us free from bondage to the positive. He grants us permission to speak about evil, suffering, hardship, and sin. His promises allow us to call a spade a

spade—to call evil evil and suffering suffering. We do not have
to pretend that it does not exist or depend upon our own supposed power to fix it. Rather, in all of it we cling to what *God*
has spoken—his promises in Christ.

Consider, for example, the exhortations given to us to confess our sins—something the Word-Faith teaching expressly
forbids. After all, if you speak your sins, you are conceding that
you are a sinner. You are changing your reality for the worse,
they say. And yet the apostle John says just the opposite: "If we
say we have no sin, we deceive ourselves, and the truth is not in
us. If we confess our sins, [God] is faithful and just to forgive
us our sins and to cleanse us from all unrighteousness" (1 John
1:8-9). John tells us to confess our sins precisely so that *God* can
change our reality. He uses his words—which actually *are* powerful to create reality—to declare us forgiven, righteous, and
holy in Christ. To avoid "sin talk" because you think it might
make you sinful is to deceive no one but yourself.

And what about the other kinds of suffering we encounter
in the world? While the Word-Faith teacher would have you
use your words to fix these things—and then blame you for
your lack of faith when your words fail—God does things differently. God does not give us answers or reasons for the suffering that we encounter. He gives us promises. Promises that are
sufficient to deliver his mercy and forgiveness. Put another way,
God gives us a way to endure suffering. He speaks into your suffering when it leaves you speechless. He promises that it will not
last forever. Christ will return on the last day to finally put it all
under his feet, where it will be finally and forever gone (1 Corinthians 15:25).

Let's keep speaking those promises in Christ to one another. They will bring far more comfort than any of our made-up mantras ever will.

Chapter 11

God Loves Social Justice

*The King will answer them, "Truly, I say to you, as you did it
to one of the least of these my brothers, you did it to me."*

MATTHEW 25:40

Consider the Claim

Do you got a Bible?" I had been a pastor for only a few weeks,
and sitting across from me in my office was George. George was
a homeless man in the city who carried around a bucket, spray
bottle, and squeegee, prepared at a moment's notice to wash
windows or scrape the bugs off your car's windshield. He also
recited poetry for freewill donations and sold handmade trin-
kets and charms.

This was the third time I had seen George in my office. He
had come, once again, requesting help, money, food, employ-
ment, or shelter. I had helped him as I was able the first two
times, but this time I was not able to. Every time I had seen him,
I had directed our conversation towards the gospel of Christ. I

tried to help him see his sin and his need for salvation. He was never opposed to the conversation, but it was clearly not his biggest concern. To him, I was just another potential dispenser of resources.

When I told him on that day that I would not be dispensing any resources to him this time—except for the free promises of Christ—he got visibly agitated.

"Do you got a Bible?"

"Of course I have a Bible. I'm a pastor," I replied.

"Lemme see it."

I reached for the Bible on my desk and handed it to him. He took some time to fumble through the thin pages with his calloused fingers that poked through his fingerless gloves. Finally, he arrived at the passage he was seeking. He turned the Bible in my direction, pointed at the spot on the page and insisted, "Read that." It was Matthew 25:45-46: "Then he will answer them, saying, 'Truly, I say to you, as you did not do it to one of the least of these, you did not do it to me.' And these will go away into eternal punishment, but the righteous into eternal life."

George waited patiently for me to comprehend the horrifying reality that Jesus was going to consign me to hell for my lack of giving him a handout. The Bible was clear. I owed him. It was my God-ordained duty to fulfill George's request. Unless, of course, I was content with the fires of hell and damnation.

I was incredibly tempted to show George his hypocrisy by using his method of interpretation against him: "Well, the Bible says to love your neighbor as yourself. It's not very loving to interrupt my busy day with your third request for help, now is it? Doesn't the Bible say that if a man isn't willing to work, then he shouldn't eat?" There were other Bible verses that he clearly did not consider authoritative, probably because he could not twist them to his own advantage. But that discussion would have been fruitless. I simply maintained that on that day I would not be able to help him, that I was always willing to pray with and for him, and that he was always welcome to come to our services and Bible studies to hear of the greatest thing he needed: the salvation and forgiveness of Jesus.

George did come around now and again. I would help him when I could, but always stressed that the most important thing he needed was the gospel of Christ. But his visits slowed down over time. Ultimately, he was not interested in joining a community of faith to receive the greatest nourishment that he needed: the forgiveness of Christ for sinners. For him, the church was just a group of hypocritical people that did not actually believe what Jesus taught about helping the homeless.

Unfortunately, many churches have taken the same sort of perspective as George. They have become nothing more than social justice warriors who justify their positions with texts like Matthew 25:31-46, but do not consider other, less popular texts as authoritative or important (for example, when Jesus claims to be the exclusive way to salvation and eternal life).

In too many instances, such churches lose sight of their purpose for existing. Christ has given his church a word of law and promise that no one else on planet Earth can proclaim. If the church doesn't do it, who will? And yet, too many are far too comfortable setting aside the faithful proclamation of God's Word and instead, doing things that many other people and organizations already do: food pantries, homeless shelters, special interest groups, and the like, all in the name of outreach. (Please do not misunderstand me. Such things are not inherently wrong, and the church is free to engage in them. I am simply pointing out that lots of organizations other than the church do such things; *no one else* is proclaiming the gospel. Only the church does that.)

On the one hand, I can see where they are coming from. A careless reading of Matthew 25:31-46 does imply that one of the most important things a church can do is to care for the down-and-out, to give shelter to the homeless, to be advocates for the weak, sick, and imprisoned. But it does not stop there. The flipside of the coin—which is usually absent from these conversations—is that if a church is *not* engaging in such social justice, then God has prepared for them nothing but hell and damnation.

Consider the Context

Matthew 25:31-46 falls at the very end of a teaching in the Gospel that has come to be known as Christ's "eschatological discourse." *Eschatology* is the study of the end times. So, in Matthew 24–25, Jesus is teaching about the end times, and it is not pretty. The temple will be destroyed (24:1-2)—a remarkable and harrowing statement, since the temple had been the center of God's dealings with his people since the time of Moses and the tabernacle (cf. Exodus 26). Of course, ultimately the true temple—Christ himself—would not be destroyed (cf. John 2:18-22). The disciples are to be on guard, since false christs will arise to deceive them (Matthew 24:4-5,11,23-27). Wars, rumors of wars, and nations locked in combat will be the sign that the birth pangs of the end have begun (24:6-8).

There is much that we could discuss in Matthew 24, but let's focus on the three parables in chapter 25. With each parable, we gain more and more insight into what Christ would have us understand concerning these gray and latter days. The first is the famous parable of the ten young maidens (25:1-13). The maidens all await the arrival of the bridegroom, so that they can enter into the wedding feast and celebrate. Five of them are wise, in that they have diligent foresight. They bring extra oil for their lamps just in case the bridegroom was delayed. The other five, however, are foolish. They have no foresight and no extra oil. When the bridegroom finally arrives after being delayed, the five wise maidens are ready to enter the feast. The five foolish ones, however, are left outside staring at a closed door. The point of this parable, it seems, is that as Christ's disciples eagerly anticipate his return, they are to be prepared, because they do not know the precise time when he will come. They are not to fall away (24:10) or be misled (24:11), but rather they are to endure to the end (24:13).

If the first parable exhorts Christ's disciples to be prepared for his coming, the second parable teaches them what they are to do in the meantime. In the parable of the talents (25:14-30), a master has gone on a journey. But before he leaves, he entrusts his talents into the care and stewardship of his servants (25:15).[3] The expectation is that they will invest their master's talents so that when he returns, he will receive back what he gave them, plus interest (25:27). The first two servants are diligent to do precisely that (25:16-17). The third servant, however, does absolutely nothing with the single talent his master gave him (25:18). Upon the master's return, the first two servants are given even more to oversee (25:21-23), but the third is thrown into the outer darkness (25:30). The point here is that Christ's disciples are not simply to rest on their laurels, as it were, as they await his return. They are to be salt and light (Matthew 5:13-14), serving their neighbors in love and proclaiming the excellencies of God (1 Peter 2:9).

This brings us to the parable that George had pointed to in my Bible. It is often called a parable, but that is not so clear. Jesus does not begin with his typical, "The kingdom of heaven is like…" After exhorting them to be prepared for his return and showing them what they are to do in the meantime, in this description Jesus assures his disciples that the Son of Man will make good on his promise; he will indeed return, and it will culminate in the judgment of all people.

I would invite you to avoid quickly skimming through Matthew 25:31-46. I am going to take more time treating this text than I do in the other chapters of this book. Stick with me, and let's walk through the text carefully to notice the details that help us understand what Jesus is saying—and what he is not saying.

First, notice who is included in this judgment. "All the nations" will be gathered before him (25:32). No one is exempt. The first order of business is to separate them out. There are sheep (an image used throughout Scripture to describe the people of God) and there are goats. Sheep will take their place on his right—the place of righteousness and salvation—and goats will be on his left—the opposite of the right (25:33). Notice that the King does not need to look at a ledger of works and merits to determine which group a person belongs to, as is so often depicted in cartoons of St. Peter at the gate of heaven consulting his big book of good works, determining the fate of each person in the endless line of people waiting to come in. No, right from the start, the sheep and goats are already clearly delineated.

Then the King speaks, first to the sheep, and his words are glorious gospel: "Come, you who are blessed by my Father, inherit the kingdom prepared for you from the foundation of the world" (25:34). The word *blessed* in Matthew's gospel carries salvation overtones in it. To be blessed is to have been made a part of Christ's kingdom by his mercy (cf. Matthew 5:1-11; 16:17). These sheep are precisely that: blessed by the Father. Therefore, they now receive the inheritance of Christ. They are not receiving wages for their work, as if they have earned God's kingdom. No, they receive what has been prepared *for them* from the foundation of the world: an inheritance (which means someone had to die in order for them to receive it; that is how inheritances work).

The King continues, and this is the part that is most often misquoted: "For I was hungry and you gave me food, I was thirsty and you gave me drink, I was a stranger and you welcomed me, I was naked and you clothed me, I was sick and you visited me, I was in prison and you came to me" (25:35-36). This is remarkable, especially when you connect it with the two preceding parables. Somehow, these blessed sheep fed, clothed, visited, and cared for this hungry, naked, sick, and imprisoned King. There is only one problem: the King was apparently gone. He had departed on a long journey and was delayed in his return. This conundrum explains the question posed by the sheep. "Lord, when did we see you hungry and feed you, or thirsty and give you drink? And when did we see you a stranger and welcome you, or naked and clothe you? And when did we see you sick or in prison and visit you" (25:37-39)?

How remarkable! The sheep were ignorant of the good works they had been performing in service to the King. They had no idea what he was talking about. They were simply doing what sheep do. But to whom did they do it? The King reveals the answer. "Truly, I say to you, as you did it to one of the least of these my brothers, you did it to me" (25:40).

Once again, we must slow down and consider a detail in that statement. The King says that the sheep had been performing these works of love for his "brothers," and therefore had been showing love to him. These "brothers" of the King are not the generic "brotherhood of mankind." No, Jesus had taught elsewhere that his brothers were those who did the will of his Father in heaven (Matthew 12:46-50). He had also taught that whoever would receive his apostles would also receive him, and therefore the one who sent him (Matthew 10:40). To hear the apostles of Christ preach was to hear the very word of Christ himself (Luke 10:16).

The brothers that had been served by these sheep were fellow Christians, especially those who had been charged to proclaim the gospel—work that would be largely rejected by those who heard it. The disciples would suffer hunger, thirst, nakedness, danger, sword, imprisonment, and death for proclaiming Christ. And those are the very maladies that elicited care of the sheep for these servants of Christ. Why? To earn some eternal reward? Not at all. Rather, because they are *already* sheep, and therefore rejoice in God's Word. Sheep see to it that those who proclaim that Word would be taken care of so that the Word may continue to go forth.

Now the King turns to the goats. His words are quite sobering: "Depart from me, you cursed, into the eternal fire prepared for the devil and his angels" (25:41). Notice that the sheep had a place prepared for them by the Father. We might expect the same to be true for the goats. But God has not prepared the eternal fire for the goats. No, he has prepared it for the devil and his angels. Now it also becomes the eternal home of those who lacked faith in Christ and his Word. And how does such unbelief manifest itself? The King says, "For I was hungry and you gave me no food, I was thirsty and you gave me no drink, I was a stranger and you did not welcome me, naked and you did not clothe me, sick and in prison and you did not visit me" (25:42-43).

This surprises the goats. "Lord, when did we see you hungry or thirsty or a stranger or naked or sick or in prison, and did not minister to you" (25:44)? Apparently these goats were keeping track of their service. Or at the very least, they are convinced that if the King had been in their midst, they *certainly* would have noticed and done all of those things and more to help him. The trouble is, he *was* in their midst and they failed to love him. "Truly, I say to you, as you did not do it to one of the least of these, you did not do it to me" (25:45). They apparently refused to hear the word preached by Christ's servants, and therefore refused to hear Christ himself.

Can you see that this whole account is not a generic teaching about how we are to be Christ's social justice warriors? It is certainly not a text to be used by the marginalized to show how they deserve special treatment from others. This text has to do with joyfully receiving the Word of God spoken through his servants, and using our time and resources to make sure that proclamation continues to go forth by caring for those who proclaim it. Why? Paul says it best: "How then will they call on him in whom they have not believed? And how are they to believe in him of whom they have never heard? And how are they to hear without someone preaching? And how are they to preach unless they are sent? As it is written, 'How beautiful are the feet of those who preach the good news!'" (Romans 10:14-15).

Consider the Comfort

If this text is teaching us that our performance in service to the hungry, thirsty, estranged, naked, sick, or imprisoned is what earns for us either salvation or damnation, then the verdict is clear: no one would be saved. No one has fulfilled that expectation perfectly, and so we would all be cast into the lake of fire prepared for the devil and all his angels. And even if we *do* spend our time exhausting ourselves serving everyone that we can, how much service is enough to merit salvation? Such a reading will inevitably turn us into goats, constantly keeping track of our service to others, not because they need our service but because we are trying to save our own skin.

However, when we read this text carefully, we see that the works performed by the sheep and the goats were simply borne out of their identity. The sheep did "sheepish" works, not in order to become sheep, but because they already were. And the same is true of the goats.

Sometimes I use an image to teach this text that I think is helpful. Imagine you have a tree that is bearing rotten fruit. One of your neighbors comes along and says, "I have just the solution for that." He rummages around in his bag and digs out a roll of duct tape and a bunch of healthy fruit. "Just take this fruit and tape it onto the tree branches. It will look as good as new!"

Of course, you know what will happen. The tree will not magically start bearing healthy fruit. It may look healthy externally for a time (aside from the duct tape), but eventually the fruit that you attach to it will itself become rotten. The problem is not with the fruit. The problem is with the tree.

As Jesus says, "Either make the tree good and its fruit good, or make the tree bad and its fruit bad, for the tree is known by its fruit" (Matthew 12:33). We cannot turn ourselves into worthy candidates for salvation simply by tacking on a bunch of good works over our wicked and sinful hearts (Matthew 15:10-20). No, our hearts themselves must be made good, and then good fruit will follow.

I hope you are not hearing me say that our works are pointless—that the hungry, thirsty, estranged, naked, and imprisoned are not worthy of our love and care. I am not saying that at all, and we will deal with that question in the next chapter. Clearly Christ expects us to hear these words and abide by them. However, what I am saying is that your works—the fruit that you bear—do not earn for you God's favor or eternal salvation. That has been done for you in Christ. And he comes to do something far more than give you a program of works by which to abide. He comes to make you a brand-new creation (2 Corinthians 5:17). He comes and clothes you in *his* works in

order to make you righteous, precisely because you could not
do it yourself.

Now, what is the result of having been made a new creation?
You go about loving and serving the neighbors in your midst,
especially (but not exclusively) those of the household of faith
(Galatians 6:10). Not to keep track of your deeds. Not to please
God. Not to earn another tally mark in St. Peter's giant book
of good works. Not to jump on the bandwagon of every single
social justice trend that may flash across the television screen.[4]
But simply to serve, as you are able, those who need service. And
as we serve, we are given opportunities to proclaim the message
that only we can: that Christ has died, risen, and is returning to
save sinners such as you and me.

Chapter 12

We Are Not Saved by Faith Alone

You see that a person is justified by works and not by faith alone.

JAMES 2:24

Consider the Claim

I do not remember his name, but I remember his face. I can still picture him smiling at me from the photo that adorned the church's promotional material. He stands there in a Western-style brown polyester suit, his large Bible open in his left hand, with his right hand resting on the pages.

He was a pastor at a local Church of Christ congregation. I say pastor. He reminded me every so often that such creatures—and the man-made institutions that create them—are not biblical. He was a preacher. A preacher of the true Word of God. In fact, we will just call him Preacher from now on. Preacher and I had met at a debate that he hosted between himself and a Seventh-day Adventist scholar. Through a series of conversations, he and I and a couple of Adventist pastors started meeting to discuss theology. Go ahead. Get the jokes out of the way right now. Two Adventists, a preacher, and a Lutheran pastor walk into a bar. It doesn't even need a punch line.

I liked Preacher. He clearly knew the information in the Bible very well and he had a firebrand quality about him that made him fun to talk with. He did not like creeds or formulated confessions, both of which I have publicly said I would die for (contained in the Book of Concord published in 1580, if you're curious). Not him. He had "no creed but the Bible." I always thought that was an interesting creed to confess.

At one of our meetings, the conversation centered around how man is justified—put in a right standing before God. It is no secret that, as a Lutheran, I gladly confess that mankind is justified before God by grace, through faith, in Jesus Christ alone, apart from our works. Not a single ounce of our effort earns God's favor for us; we cannot merit Christ's forgiveness in the slightest. I said as much in our little meeting.

Preacher got quite animated at that statement. "If you do a search on your fancy computer software for the words 'faith alone,' you will come up with only one result in all of the Bible. James 2:24." Gesturing at me he continued, "I'm sure you're not happy to learn that James 2:24 clearly says that man is *not* saved by faith alone, but by works." It was weird. He seemed to think I had never read James and that this was brand new information to me.

Unfortunately, our meetings only lasted a few months. None of us was convinced of the others' positions. Not only were all of our schedules very busy, but it also became clear that we were not making any headway. The combination of those two things resulted in us going our separate ways.

Even so, I cherish those few meetings that we had together because it gave me a chance to sharpen my confession by being driven back to the Word of God. Every single one of our conversations—like all of theology—centered around this most important question: how is a sinful and unrighteous person made right before the one, true, perfect, holy, and almighty God?

There are plenty of Scriptures that teach us of the great mercy of Christ for sinful humanity who are unable to save themselves. There are passages that clearly proclaim the doctrine of justification, which some have described as "the doctrine on which the church stands or falls." Salvation is not by works but by faith in Christ. Then James 2:24 comes along, which, read all by itself, seems to contradict them all.

Consider the Context

When discussing the relationship between faith and works, it is all too easy to get the proverbial cart before the horse. This is a conversation that theologians and scholars have wrestled with and argued about for millennia, ever since apostolic days.

On one extreme are those who have blatantly said that salvation is attained by some combination of man's work and God's work. Some say that man gets things started and God, seeing that potential, fills in the rest. Others say that God gets things started and now it is man's job to keep the ball rolling.

On the other extreme are those who confess that because

salvation cannot be merited by good works, therefore good works no longer play a role in the Christian life. When Scripture exhorts people to holy living, the sole purpose, they would say, is to show the unattainable standard God has set. Unable to meet such a standard, we then despair of our inability to perform such demanding good works, and therefore we are driven to rejoice again in the free salvation won by Christ, who has set us free from good works. The fancy term for such a perspective is *antinomianism,* which literally means "against the law."

However, the biblical witness—including James—militates against both of these extremes. Just consider some of the texts that clearly proclaim that we are saved by grace through faith. I would invite you to look them up and read them for yourself in context.

Ephesians 2:1-10—Here Paul explicitly says that God is the one who makes us alive with Christ and that this is a gift that is not our own doing.

John 1:12-13—John speaks about people "receiving" and "believing in" Christ here. But he is quick to say that such children of God are born, "not of blood nor of the will of the flesh nor of the will of man, but of God."

Romans 3:21-28—Paul beautifully proclaims that the righteousness we have before God is given to us through faith in Jesus Christ and that this justification is a pure gift. A person, says Paul, is made righteous by faith apart from works of the law.

Romans 10:13-17—Verse 13, by itself, could imply that man's initial work is to call upon the name of the Lord in order to be saved. But notice the progression that Paul gives as the text continues. In order to call upon the Lord's name, one must *first* believe in the Lord. And to believe, someone must *first* preach to them. And in order for someone to preach, that person must *first* be sent with the Word of Christ, through which faith comes. It is God, preaching his Word through his servants, who creates the faith that allows a person to call upon the name of the Lord.

And, lest we think that the act of believing is itself a work that we perform, consider these:

Romans 4:1-5—Here Paul uses Abraham as an example of someone who was given the gift of faith. Abraham did not earn the saving wages that were his due by performing the works of the law. In these verses, *either* a person works for his salvation, and therefore the salvation is not a gift, *or* the salvation is a free gift that creates saving faith, and a person does not work for it. Paul excludes the possibility that saving faith itself can be a work that we perform.

John 6:28-29—In this part of a lengthy discourse, the Jews ask Jesus, "What must we do, to be doing the works of God?" Jesus gives a remarkable response. "This is the work of God, that you believe in him whom he has sent." Apparently our believing in Christ is something that God accomplishes, not us.

So what about James and his comments about faith and works? Is he blatantly denying what the above verses—and many others—say?

Well, no. In fact, to understand what James is saying is pretty straightforward if we read chapter 2 in light of chapter 1, specifically James 1:18.

In 1:1-15 James clearly exhorts and encourages fellow Christians to stand up under the trials and temptations of the world and their flesh. He calls them "my brothers" and refers to "the testing of your faith." Apparently the recipients of this letter were already Christians. If they were unbelievers, James would not refer to them as his brothers (1:2,16), they would not have a faith to be tested (1:3), nor would he exhort them to pray to God in faith for wisdom (1:5-8). And in 1:18 James clearly understands that they have been made Christians purely by the work of God's Word: "*Of his own will* he brought us forth by the word of truth…"

Whatever James says, he says it to people who have already received the gift of saving faith. The problem that James addresses is not how people are converted from unbelief to belief. Rather, the issue at hand is this: What if people who have saving faith say that, because of such faith, they do not need to perform good works? What happens when Christians become antinomian?

James's answer is that the Christian life ought to be full of the fruit of good works. The whole letter is replete with exhortations to holy living and good works, and rightly so. The gospel bears much fruit in the Christian's life as he goes about diligently serving the people that God has placed in his midst. Christians are to be doers of the word (1:22). Christians are to bridle their tongues (1:26; 3:1-12) and care for the weak and lowly in their midst (1:27). Christians are not to evaluate people using outward, worldly standards (2:1-13) nor live according to worldly wisdom (3:13–4:17).

Do not misunderstand. James is not telling these Christians how to stay saved, as if maintaining their salvation depends upon doing good works. Instead he is exposing their misunderstanding of what it means to be a Christian. A good tree does not bear bad fruit. Therefore, you cannot claim that you are a good tree and despise the good fruit that a good tree ought to bear.

The apostle Paul says something similar in Romans 6. After spending two and a half chapters declaring the beautiful gospel that we are saved by no works of our own, Paul anticipates what the sinful flesh might say. "Well that's pretty neat. God likes to forgive. I like to sin. We make a great team." Paul addresses this misunderstanding. "Should we go on sinning so that grace may abound? May it never be!" Such an attitude is, in fact, to despise the gospel of Christ.

So then, we are left with the question of the proper place of good works in the Christian's life. Good works flow out of having been saved by grace through faith in Jesus Christ alone. They are not for God's benefit but for our neighbors'. Our good works do not save us. But neither do Christians get to claim that they have been set free from sin and death by the gospel, and then turn around and despise their neighbor and the good works that God has prepared for us to walk in (Ephesians 2:10). Faith and works go together. We simply must keep them in the right order.

Consider the Comfort

I remember having a couple of Mormon missionaries in my home one evening. We spoke for at least an hour about faith, works, and how we obtain righteousness before God. I kept on pointing them to passages in the Bible that proclaim the glorious good news that Christ has come to accomplish salvation for us—that every requirement of the law has been fulfilled in his life, death, and resurrection from the dead.

The young missionaries, however, kept pointing me to a verse from the Book of Mormon that says that a man is saved by grace after all he can do (2 Nephi 25:23). The remarkable thing to me is that this struck their ears as good news. They would try their hardest and then God would fill in the gaps. It would all work out in the end. (Actually, I remember Preacher saying something similar in one of our conversations.)

So I posed some questions to them: Has there ever been a time when your neighbor was in need and you didn't help them? While you were sleeping last night, was there anyone that could have used your help, but you continued to slumber while they suffered? Have you ever had a wicked thought about someone rather than love them and consider how you could serve them? Do you ever take time off just to relax, while there are people around you who require your service? They were honest fellows, and so they answered, "Yes." So I simply replied, "Then it sounds to me like you *haven't* done all that you can do. So now what?"

They had never even considered that. All they could say was, "We'll have to think about that." They simply assumed that their best was good enough and that they had, in fact, been doing their best. But they hadn't. No one has. And such thinking is not unique to those Mormon missionaries. That is the temptation of us all—to lower the bar of God's perfect standard and to conclude that we have measured up.

However, there is no certainty of salvation nor comfort in a theology that teaches that we are saved by our works. The only way to operate in such a religion is to constantly be pointing at everyone who appears less righteous than yourself, so that you can prove that you are at least better than they are. You may have your mistakes, but you are not as bad as the next person. And yet the nagging question never goes away: have I done enough? And the answer is always a despairing no.

That is why it is such incredible news to hear that we are saved by grace through faith in Christ alone, period. It has all been done for us. And what is equally remarkable is that such promises actually set us free to serve our neighbors in joy. Christ has freely saved us, not so that we do not have to do good works. Rather, because Christ has freely saved us, we are set free to do good works without worrying whether our status before God depends upon our performance. We find ourselves desiring to serve those around us and to perform good works, not so that we would be saved and forgiven by Jesus, but because we already are.

Such was the case for Abraham and Rahab, the two examples used by James (2:21-26). Both of them performed their good works as people who had already been given the promises of God. And so it is with the Christian.

We no longer have to run on the rat wheel of constantly trying to keep God pleased with us through our efforts. We can put down the mental tally sheet that keeps a record of our good works so that we can show them proudly to God. We can stop trying to make ourselves look good by comparing ourselves to the people around us who are obviously more sinful. Instead, we can freely go about serving our neighbors simply because they are our neighbors, because through Christ we already know where we stand with our Father in heaven.

Chapter 13

Christ Is Your Copilot

I can do all things through [Christ] who strengthens me.

PHILIPPIANS 4:13

Consider the Claim

It has adorned too many a weight-room wall: a poster sporting toned biceps, triceps, calves, quads, and abs. Weights and lifting equipment enhance the background. And there, in bold, motivational type: "I can do ALL THINGS through Christ who STRENGTHENS me." There is nothing like the comfort of Christ, who helps you endure the burn while you strive for that perfect, beach-worthy bod.

It has been printed in countless greeting cards displaying a mountainous backdrop as a backpacker looks across the rugged landscape that she is determined to conquer. "I can do all things through Christ who strengthens me." The greeting card marks the completion of one of life's chapters. The really good aunts affix said greeting card to a shiny copy of Dr. Seuss's *Oh, the*

Places You'll Go! Whether you have graduated from preschool, kindergarten, eighth grade, high school, or college, have no fear. You will be able to do anything in life you set your mind to and scale any obstacle in your way. Why? Because your strength is Christ. (Although, should you decide to traverse those rugged mountain trails depicted on the greeting card, your strength in Christ should not deter you from packing healthy rations of protein bars, water, and a first-aid kit.)

It has been quoted by some medal-winning Olympians who respond to the question, "What are you feeling right now?" with a laborious, out-of-breath, "I can do all things through Christ who strengthens me!" and a finger extended to the heavens to give credit where credit is due.

To be sure, such a use of this verse is incredibly inspirational. Who doesn't love to hear that God has their back in all the endeavors they undertake? Philippians 4:13, used like this, has a way of sanctifying our goals, making the deepest passions of our hearts holy, noble, and godly things to pursue with the strength of Christ undergirding it all. (As an aside, do a quick search for the word *passion* in the Bible. There is not a single reference where our passions are considered good, God-given things.) But here's the thing: while it is meant to make us focus on Christ, such a use of this verse makes Christ a footnote to our great achievements; it always draws attention to those people and situations that the world considers great.

But as inspirational as it sounds on a poster or in a greeting card, the reality of life constantly contradicts this popular use of Philippians 4:13. Just consider your own life. At some point in your existence, you have set goals and striven for your aspirations, perhaps to discover that you often are not disciplined enough to reach them. When faced with such disappointment in yourself, Christ becomes nothing more than a morning dose of caffeine, a spiritual steroid, your life coach who will believe in you when no one else does. Or, even worse, perhaps you try your hardest to accomplish your dreams and make them come true, firmly believing Philippians 4:13, but alas, you never quite get there. Not because you didn't give it your all, but because—and this is the scary thought—perhaps Christ was not with you in it. Go through *that* enough times and the "Christ who strengthens me" starts to seem like the Christ who is happy to let me crash and burn. Eventually the best mantra you can muster is, "I can sort of do some things through Christ who strengthens me, when and where he gets around to it."

Thankfully, there is a better way. But to see that, you must first see the good news that Philippians 4:13 is about Christ before it is about you.

Consider the Context

The apostle Paul had one goal in life, and even that one was not of his own making. It was given to him by the crucified and risen Christ in a literally blinding flash of light on the Damascus road (Acts 9:1-19). The man who persecuted Christians unto death was incredibly commissioned by Jesus to be perhaps his greatest witness. Ever since that day, the apostle's goal was this: to proclaim the pure gospel of Christ. Paul was not on a six-month plan, a five-year plan, or a ten-year plan. We do not have any record that Paul, concerned about his weight, was on a special diet (except where it served the gospel; cf. 1 Corinthians

8–10), or that he held himself to a rigid exercise schedule. No, Paul's goal was simple and straightforward. Just consider a sample of what he himself writes:

> I am under obligation both to Greeks and to barbarians, both to the wise and to the foolish. So I am eager to preach the gospel to you also who are in Rome. For I am not ashamed of the gospel, for it is the power of God for salvation to everyone who believes, to the Jew first and also to the Greek (Romans 1:14-16).

> I, when I came to you, brothers, did not come proclaiming to you the testimony of God with lofty speech or wisdom. For I decided to know nothing among you except Jesus Christ and him crucified (1 Corinthians 2:1-2).

> If I preach the gospel, that gives me no ground for boasting. For necessity is laid upon me. Woe to me if I do not preach the gospel! For if I do this of my own will, I have a reward, but if not of my own will, I am still entrusted with a stewardship. What then is my reward? That in my preaching I may present the gospel free of charge, so as not to make full use of my right in the gospel (1 Corinthians 9:16-18).

> If we or an angel from heaven should preach to you a gospel contrary to the one we preached to you, let him be accursed. As we have said before, so now I say again: If anyone is preaching to you a gospel contrary to the one you received, let him be accursed. For am I now seeking the approval of man, or of God? Or am I

trying to please man? If I were still trying to please man,
I would not be a servant of Christ (Galatians 1:8-10).

Paul, along with the rest of the apostles, was given an incredible responsibility and privilege: they were entrusted with the
only message in the universe that gives true life. But such a
charge to proclaim the pure gospel would also bring with it
hardship (Acts 9:16). Paul was not out to scratch itching ears
(2 Timothy 4:3-4). The message he brought was offensive and
foolish (1 Corinthians 1:23) and his preaching got him chased
out of town more than once (Acts 9:23-25,29-30; 13:50; 14:5-
7). During his journeys to proclaim the cross and empty tomb,
he endured all manner of suffering (2 Corinthians 11:16-28),
including the famous thorn in his flesh (2 Corinthians 12:7)
and eventual martyrdom.

It is within this context—suffering for the sake of the gospel—that Paul writes Philippians 4:13. Consider what he says
right before it. Paul is thankful for the Christians at Philippi
because they have revived their concern for him (4:10). They
have supported him in his ministry, likely in a financial way, and
for that he is thankful. But he is also quick to add that, even if
they had not contributed to support his needs—even if he were
starving and at the lowest point regarding his physical needs—
he would still rejoice and be content. Why? Because Christ is
his strength, and so he can endure all things—even the most
difficult suffering.

Consider the Comfort

The pastoral ministry has taken me into some pretty difficult places. I have heard people confess sins from decades past

that still gnaw and make the conscience raw. I have sat at the bedsides of dying parishioners, striving to bring the Word of God into the valley of death's shadow, sometimes fighting to be heard over the chillingly loud rattle in their chest as they breathe their last. I have striven to use God's Word alone to convince the wayward and erring so that they would not remain in despair and unbelief.

In all of these difficult circumstances, it would be utter foolishness to urge such people simply to try harder and work harder to achieve their goals. That kind of proclamation sounds good and appealing when suffering is far off. But when death's sting is sharp and imminent, when despair and doubt hang over you like a cloud and suffering will not let up, greeting card sentiments prove themselves to be empty drivel. In those moments what you need above all is not a motivational mantra. You need Christ. Not as a life coach. Not as a self-esteem booster. Not as a band-aid to fix your problems. Not as a footnote to your great, inspirational life story. But as your sufficient Savior from sin, death, and the power of the devil.

You see, when we take this verse off the poster on the weight-room wall, when we strip it of its greeting card sentimentality, when we stop quoting it only when we have achieved something the world considers great, when we stop making it all about us and our achievements and instead all about Christ and his mercy, then we can bring it with us even into the pit of suffering and rejoice in its comfort.

Paul knows that no amount of temporal suffering can outweigh the eternal prize that awaits him on the last day (Romans 8). Far from being a simple motivational mantra encouraging you to aim high and strive for earthly dreams, Philippians 4:13 is a promise that Christ and all his gifts are enough for you, even if your life seems to be crumbling around you. Yes, even then you can endure and be content, not on account of your own strength but from the strength that comes from the word that is eternal in the heavens: Christ is and always will be crucified and risen even for you. And that is enough.

Chapter 14

Overcome Debt, Depression, and Other Goliaths in Your Life

David prevailed over the Philistine with a sling and with a stone, and struck the Philistine and killed him. There was no sword in the hand of David.

1 SAMUEL 17:50

Consider the Claim

On his program *Fighting for the Faith*, Pastor Chris Rosebrough teaches biblical discernment by discussing sermons, teachings, and popular Christian books. He helps the listener wade through the multitude of false preaching and teaching that blares over the airwaves and internet bandwidth. One of the most common errors that he points out in popular preaching and teaching is what he calls "narcigesis." The word is a mash-up of *narcissism*—being utterly enamored with oneself—and *exegesis*—the discipline of correct biblical study. The "narcigete" is the person who, rather than drawing out the meaning that the text itself gives, will instead insert himself into the text wherever he can manage, importing meaning that was not there before.

It is an exciting way to read the Bible, really, to see yourself on every page. The narcigete is not terribly concerned with what the words of a text mean in their context, nor is he even concerned with the historicity of the biblical narrative. If anything, the words of Scripture are simply a springboard from which he can launch himself into all manner of interpretation. All that matters to him is where he can learn a life lesson or daily application from any and every text he encounters. "How is this text about me?" he asks of every verse he finds. Some texts require some creative finagling before the narcigete finds a crack into which his ego can slip. Other texts are rife with opportunity for the narcigete to barge in unannounced. David and Goliath is one of those texts.

On one side we have the young, underdog shepherd boy, David. On the other side we have the great, mighty, javelin-toting, armor-bearing, blaspheming Philistine named Goliath. Everyone on Israel's side is too scared to fight this formidable champion warrior. But faithful David offers himself as the worthy opponent.

David is too small to wear armor, so he equips himself with nothing more than a staff, five smooth stones, and a sling. You know the story. After some mockery from Goliath, the two approach each other. David slings a stone squarely into his enemy's forehead, knocking him unconscious. David then beheads Goliath with his own sword. The Philistines flee. Israel plunders them. God's people win by the hand of David.

So what does it mean? An all too common interpretation begins with this question: What are the Goliaths in your life? What are the big, giant, scary things that are holding you back or pushing down upon you? Whatever they are, you must not be scared, for God is with you. So choose your smooth stones and attack the giants in your life. Is your Goliath financial trouble? Then perhaps your smooth stone is a financial advisor. Is your Goliath low self-esteem? Then maybe your smooth stone is surrounding yourself with people who will encourage you and lift you up. Is your Goliath a struggle to believe the promises of God? Then your smooth stone is to believe harder—have more reckless, relentless faith.

Notice how we are no longer talking about a real, historical Goliath who was killed by a real, historical smooth stone by a real, historical person named David. We have substituted them for something else. This sort of interpretation is called *allegorizing* the text—looking for metaphorical meaning in every single element of any given text.

Allegorizing a biblical text is not always wrong. Our Lord Jesus does this very thing when he tells a parable and then interprets it for the disciples (cf. Matthew 13:3-9,18-23; 13:24-30,36-43). However, it is not the way to deal with historical narratives, such as David and Goliath. And yet, the narcigete in all of us loves to do it, to go to work finding where we can fit ourselves into a text. It is interesting that with David and Goliath, you hardly ever hear the narcigete identify himself with the terrified, faithless Israelites. No, for the narcigete, we are always most like David, the unlikely hero.

But what if the story of David and Goliath is not about you or me? What if—like the rest of Scripture—it is about Jesus?

Consider the Context

The overarching context in which we need to understand the story of David and Goliath is that of God's kingship over his people. Way back in Genesis, God gave Abraham and his barren wife, Sarah, a promise. God would make a great nation out of Abraham, and he would do so through Abraham's son by Sarah (Genesis 17:15-16). Every nation of the earth would be blessed through Abraham (Genesis 12:3). Obviously the promise was given in the most unlikely of circumstances. Sarah was barren, after all. If this promise was going to be fulfilled, it would be God who would bring it to pass.

And he does. Isaac is born to Abraham and Sarah in their old age. To Isaac is born Jacob, who is renamed Israel (Genesis 32:28). Through Jacob the twelve tribes of Israel are born as God's chosen people, unique from any other on the planet.

One of the things that sets them apart is that they had no earthly king like the rest of the nations around them. God was their king. He was their provider and protector. He was the one who delivered them out of Egyptian slavery (Exodus 5–14). He was the one who provided for them in their wilderness wanderings (Exodus 16). He was the one who eventually brought them into the promised land that he had pledged to Abraham so long before (cf. the book of Joshua). God, Israel's powerful king, made promises and kept them. Who else did they need?

This brings us to 1 Samuel. After a period of history ruled by judges—who increasingly got more wicked as time went on—Israel was tired of the way things were going. They saw all the nations around them and wanted what they had: a king.

Israel approaches the prophet Samuel to make their request (1 Samuel 8:4-5). Samuel asks God what he should do with the request (8:6). Considering that such a request is basically saying to God, "You are failing us as king, Lord. We want someone better," God's answer to Samuel is rather surprising. "Listen to them," he says (8:7). Even though such a request was a rejection of God as their king, he would still give them what they wanted, and he promises them it will not be as great as they think. Their new king would take their sons for his army, their daughters and servants to work in his household, and their fields and vineyards for his own servants. When all this happened, then they would cry out to God, complaining to him that he gave them exactly what they asked for (8:10-18). Apparently sinners acting like petulant children is nothing new.

Their first king, Saul, was a likely candidate. His father was "a mighty man of valor" (1 Samuel 9:1 NASB). Saul was the most fetching fella in all of Israel, standing a head taller than anyone around (9:2). At the age of thirty, his reign starts out well. He is strong and competent and leads Israel to victory. However, the power seems to have gone to his head. He forgets that even he is accountable to someone greater, and he forgets the ways of God, disobeying his commands (1 Samuel 15:10-11). A new king is needed.

If Saul was the most likely candidate for a king, David was the least likely. When Samuel gets to lowly Bethlehem and tells

Jesse to bring his sons before him, Samuel takes a look at them
and thinks, "Surely the Lord's anointed is before him" (1 Samuel 16:6). But none of the seven was the man chosen by God.
No, instead, they have to call in the youngest shepherd boy
from the fields. The text tells us that he is "ruddy" and "hand-
some" with nice eyes (16:12), but obviously not anyone's first
choice. And yet this unlikely young shepherd boy would be Israel's next—and most important—earthly king.

If you know the history of Israel's kings (and Judah's, after
the split into two kingdoms), then you know that the vast
majority of them are wicked and godless. They almost go out
of their way to lead God's people into idolatry and unbelief.
There are a few here and there that bring the people back to
repentant faith, but for the most part, Israel's and Judah's kings
are lousy. But David stands out among them all, starting with
his slaying of Goliath. This unlikely shepherd boy becomes
the nation's greatest leader, precisely because he trusts God's
unfailing Word.

David is not perfect, by any stretch of the imagination. But
he is a man after God's own heart (1 Samuel 13:14). David is not
afraid to confess his sin when confronted with it (2 Samuel 12:1-
15) and to rejoice in the Lord's mercy alone (Psalm 51). Under
David's shepherding reign, Israel prospered.

And yet, there is more. David's reign does not exist as an
end in itself. It points to something greater. God seems to set
up David as a great king precisely so that he can make another
promise. As great as David is, God promises an even greater Son
to David. This descendant of David would also have a kingdom
and a throne. However, unlike David—or any other king—this

ruler's kingdom and reign would be everlasting (2 Samuel 7:8-17). From David's great line would come the greatest king ever known.

Like David, this eternal king is a humanly unlikely choice. He comes from the lowliest of places (Micah 5:2; Matthew 2:1, 23). His reign—to the chagrin of many—was not to smite anyone's earthly enemies, engage in military conquest, or rule over a grand worldly nation. Rather, he comes to wear a crown made of thorns and to rule from a throne made of wood. He holds in his hand, not a scepter gilded in gold, but nails stained in his blood. If you and I had seen Jesus that day, flogged and crucified, we would not have happily given him our allegiance. We would not have pointed to him and declared, "There is power and might!" Our human wisdom would tell us that a crucified Messiah is a failed Messiah (1 Corinthians 1:23).

And yet, God's wisdom is far above ours. His ways are greatly superior to ours. God proclaims that in this humility and weakness there is power beyond anything the world has ever known. In this death there is life. Jesus comes to reign in power over the great enemies of sin, death, and the devil, and he does it in a way that no one would've expected.

Consider the Comfort

It may seem like I have strayed a bit from the story of David and Goliath. I have. And that is okay. Because when we put the story back into the context of God accomplishing salvation through great David's greater Son, Jesus, we see that David and Goliath is just one part. We see that God accomplishes the salvation of his people despite the sinful requests of his people.

God uses their sinful request for a king to establish a kingly line through which the greatest King of all would come.

This story is not a program given to us to show us how we can overcome any given "Goliath" through the "smooth stones" of faith, resilience, or anything else that depends upon us. David's skirmish with Goliath is just one part of a much bigger, grander story of God establishing his gracious reign and rule despite the sin of his chosen people. God's mercy and grace come to us, not in great power and might, but in lowly humility.

This truth can be seen only when we stop "narcigeting" the biblical text, when we stop searching for how we can be the hero in the story. Instead, we search for Christ. We strive to see what God is up to. When we do that, we see that he is faithful to keep his gracious promises for all people, including you and me.

Chapter 15

God Believes in You

God is faithful, and he will not let you be
tempted beyond your ability.

1 Corinthians 10:13

Consider the Claim

Sharon had come to my office asking for wisdom. It turns out she just needed to pour out her concerns, fears, and frustrations. Her story was like many, I suppose. She and her husband had both grown up in the church. She faithfully attended not only Sunday services, but also midweek services and Bible studies. She loved being in God's Word.

She had also tried to pass on that love of God's Word to her son. She brought him to church, taught him to pray and love others. She did "what any good Christian parent would do," as we like to say.

But her son grew up. He made many poor decisions. He

married, had children, got divorced. The whiskey bottle became his constant companion. Anger and resentment was the language he spoke. He lost his wife, lost custody of his children, lost his job, and according to Sharon, lost his faith.

All of this brought a tidal wave of emotions upon Sharon. She was feeling guilt over what appeared to be her failed parenting. She was feeling anger at her son because he had selfishly alienated himself from everyone who loved him. She was feeling fear because she did not know if the next phone call might be from the police, telling her that he was in jail, or worse, dead. On top of it all, Sharon's husband was undergoing extreme health problems and had almost died at least twice in the last year.

When someone unleashes so many emotions into a conversation and finally breaks down in tears because they have exhausted their words, there is often silence. For me as a pastor, that silence is not only an opportunity to wade through everything that has been said, but also a blessed opportunity to simply sit with one of Christ's lambs in their grief and pain. It is to recognize that there are no silver bullet answers. Such silence is first to recognize that sin and sin's consequences still knock us to the ground and we are helpless under their weight. The creation keeps on groaning (Romans 8).

But eventually words need to be spoken. One does not simply say, "Man, that's tough. Well, I'll pray for you. Have a nice day." And so what is to be said? This time, Sharon herself broke the silence. "Well," she sniffled. "I suppose the Bible says that God doesn't give us more than we can handle. Right, pastor?"

What is to be said?

Consider the Context

It is somehow meant to be a comforting statement. The greeting card sentiment tries to make sense of the hardship and suffering that living in a sinful world brings. "God won't give you more than you can handle." I have always struggled to figure out why such a statement is comforting. First, it implies that all the suffering we endure is given by God. Second, it puts all of the onus on us to be able to handle such suffering. It is up to us to fix the problem, and since the problem has apparently been given by God, there is the added pressure of not disappointing him when we *aren't* able to handle it.

The only reason I can conjure to explain why this sentiment is comforting is that it gives a glimmer hope where there is none. There is the promise that, given enough time and hard work on our part, we will eventually overcome whatever it is that is causing us pain. In short, it promises that God has faith in us to be able to rise to the challenges of life. God will not give *us* more than *we* can handle. He really must believe in us.

If you open your Bible to find this phrase, good luck. You have a better chance of finding these words on the front of a card in the religious section of the Hallmark display at the drugstore. One of the problems with this phrase is that it sounds enough like a Bible verse that people have begun to believe that it actually *is* one. But when we compare it to the actual verse that it mimics, we discover just how empty its sentiment is.

It attempts to copy a portion of 1 Corinthians 10:13: "God is faithful, and he will not let you be tempted beyond your ability." Notice that whatever this verse is saying, it is not speaking to the person enduring suffering. Rather, it is speaking specifically to Christians experiencing temptation. And when we read the context, we learn precisely the sort of temptation Paul is speaking about.

The membership of the Corinthian church contended with a world much like our own. One of the characteristics that permeated their culture was a plurality of religious ideas and a panoply of deities to which one could offer devotion. This false worship included appeasing gods and looking for their favor by offering sacrifices as well as engaging in sexual immorality with temple prostitutes. In fact, many in the Corinthian church had come out of such pagan idol worship, which is why Paul discusses the issue of eating meat that had been sacrificed to idols (1 Corinthians 8). The idea of refraining from eating such meat was not simply to avoid offending others. Rather, the Christian brother would avoid eating such meat because to do so ran the risk of tempting the formerly pagan idolater *back into that life of false worship* that ultimately leads only to hell. Opportunities abounded for the Corinthian Christian to return to a former life of idolatry, and so they had to be especially on their guard against this very real temptation.

And that is the real issue in 1 Corinthians 10. It is not suffering in general that is under discussion. It is specifically the temptation to deny the one true God by worshiping a multitude of false ones. No one, says Paul, is immune to that temptation—not even God's chosen people. Paul says as much when he recounts some of Israel's sad history in verses 1-10.

The Israelites had been chosen and saved by God purely by his grace and mercy. In a mysterious way, Christ himself was with them even in the wilderness (v. 4). And yet, they had their fair share of failings and sin. In verse 7 he recalls how they acted as idolaters by worshiping a golden calf (Exodus 32:1-6). Verse 8 is a reminder of how they practiced sexual immorality with foreigners and worshiped their false gods (Numbers 25:1-9). Verse 9 calls to memory how, like petulant children, they faithlessly whined and grumbled after being delivered from Egyptian slavery because they had no food or water, even though they had seen the great and mighty wonders of God (Numbers 14; 21:4-9).

All of these events in the past serve as an example, a warning to God's people in the present (1 Corinthians 10:6,11). God was not afraid to render his judgment upon those who gave in to the temptation of idolatry then, and he will do the same in the present in the Corinthian congregation. "Therefore let anyone who thinks that he stands take heed lest he fall" (10:12). If you think you are unique by being tempted towards godlessness, if you think that God will go easy on you because you are special or different from someone else, think again. "No temptation has overtaken you that is not common to man" (10:13).

And yet God does not leave us to wallow helplessly in the face of temptation. Paul goes on. When we are tempted to be faithless, "God is faithful, and he will not let you be tempted beyond your ability, but with the temptation he will also provide the way of escape, that you may be able to endure it. Therefore, my beloved, flee from idolatry" (10:13-14).

This text is not about God having faith in his people to be able to handle anything he might throw their way. This text is about God's people having faith in him, especially when the temptations to do otherwise are great. The good news is that, while the temptations are great, God's mercy is greater. He is faithful. He provides the means of escape when we are tempted to disbelieve his Word and promises.

The "way of escape" can be a somewhat difficult phrase. It is not terribly specific. Paul does not say, "When you are tempted to idolatry, here is exactly how God will provide the way out for you. Step one…" However, I do believe that, once again, the context helps us out.

Immediately following this discussion of temptation to idolatry, Paul begins discussing the Lord's Supper. He starts in 10:15 and continues through the end of chapter 11. There is not sufficient space here to discuss the various denominational differences concerning the Lord's Supper. As a Lutheran, I joyfully and gladly confess that in that meal Christ mysteriously places into our mouths his true body and blood for the forgiveness of sins. I also realize that many other Christians believe differently.

However, despite our difference of confession, I do think we can say this: in the face of idolatrous temptation, Paul would encourage Christ's church to return over and again to the gifts he has given where he delivers his firm and unchanging promises. Flee idolatry. Take the way of escape that God has provided. What is that? His Word and promises that are given through Christ's shed blood for the forgiveness of sins. When false gods tempt you, return to the true God over and over and over again. Certainly one of the places where we encounter the one true God and receive his gracious promises is in the meal of the Lord's Supper.

Notice how this shifts the burden of handling temptation. Instead of relying upon our own efforts and willpower to overcome temptation, we instead return to God, who proves himself faithful time and again. Instead of God having faith in us, we trust in him to keep us in the one true faith.

Consider the Comfort

As I continued to speak with Sharon, it became clear that her concerns about her son were only part of her grief. The other part is that she was fighting against the nagging idea that God was slowly abandoning her. She was tempted to disbelieve him and his promises on account of the pain and suffering she was experiencing. She was being tempted toward idolatry.

"Well, at least God doesn't give us more than we can handle, right pastor?" After some silence, the first thing I told Sharon was, "I'm not so sure about that. We live in a sinful and broken creation, and as a result we have to endure all kinds of suffering. Sometimes we are victims of it. Sometimes we perpetrate it. We can't handle it. But God can. And God does." I went on to remind Sharon that God's promises in Christ for her do not ebb and flow with the circumstances of life. His promises are not only certain when life is good, but also—and especially—when life is bad.

This small reminder comforted her. There was no promise that things with her son would get better (although they have). There was no seven-step program to give her that would help her fix the problem. There was no encouragement that God had faith in her so she just needed to pull herself together and keep on keepin' on. No, there was simply Jesus and all of his promises, right in the middle of her sin and suffering and pain. And Jesus is enough.

Chapter 16

God Speaks to You in Whispers

Behold, the Lord *passed by, and a great and strong wind tore the mountains and broke in pieces the rocks before the* Lord, *but the* Lord *was not in the wind. And after the wind an earthquake, but the* Lord *was not in the earthquake. And after the earthquake a fire, but the* Lord *was not in the fire. And after the fire the sound of a low whisper. And when Elijah heard it, he wrapped his face in his cloak and went out and stood at the entrance of the cave. And behold, there came a voice to him…*

1 Kings 19:11-13

Consider the Claim

I never quite knew how to respond to him. Jim was a ninety-one-year-old man who had lived a full life, to say the least. He was one of the gentlest people I had ever met, soft-spoken and perpetually smiling. He and his wife could hardly make it to church, and so I would visit them in their home. I would hear the story of how they met and fell in love. He would tell me about how he worked hard in the lumber industry at the height of its success in the Pacific Northwest. Although he could barely take three steps without the aid of a walking stick, Jim had lived one of the most active, rewarding, and regret-less lives I had ever heard of.

And not only did Jim know that his life was full of blessings, he also knew from whence such blessings came. Never did I visit him when he did not speak of the great mercy of God who not only gave him the breath in his lungs, but also the pure joy to live out that gift of life to the fullest. Jim would credit God with everything that happened in his life, whether painful or not, because to him everything was either an outright blessing or a blessing in disguise.

Jim would call all of these blessings "God winks." Did the mail carrier drop off a letter from the doctor with good news? God wink. Did your granddaughter win a student of the year award for her good grades? God wink. Did the rain showers pause for a second to give you a glimpse of a ray of sunshine? God wink. Did you win the game of pinochle you were playing against your wife? God wink.

Everywhere Jim looked, there was God, communicating to him in a special and unique way that no one else could see. Every visit I had with him, Jim would retell some experience he had, and at the end of every story he would look at me with a glimmer in his eye and his smile growing as he pointed his finger at me and gleefully declared, "God wink!"

I would be lying if I said there wasn't a certain appeal to Jim's

God winks. He had lived an amazing life, after all, and had apparently noticed God's hand in every tiny detail. Could he see something that I had missed? Did God speak more to him than he had to me? What did I have to do to receive my own winks from God?

I always tried to interpret his experiences, pointing him to the clear and certain promises that God has declared in Christ, promises that are true regardless of who wins the pinochle game.

Jim's perspective was not inherently wrong. I believe it was just his way of giving thanks to God in all circumstances (1 Thessalonians 5:18). However, his perspective is a small example of a far bigger problem that has taken root in Christ's church. It is the idea that God speaks to every single person on the planet in completely different ways—that God gives individual, unique, immediate revelation to people through prophecy, visions, dreams, circumstances, intuitions, feelings, and extraordinary manifestations of the Spirit. God winks, if you will.

So pervasive is this idea that it has become not only assumed but nearly unquestionable. To begin to question this view of God inevitably invites the criticism that the questioner is "boxing in the Spirit" or "putting limits upon God." In fact, I used to say those very same things. "Who am I to say what God can or cannot do? Who do I think I am to dictate how he can or cannot communicate to us?" God can do anything he wants, I thought, which therefore opened the door to all manner of places that God might reveal himself.

However, what ultimately changed my mind on the matter was the lack of comfort and certainty. In that way of thinking, if I was going to be honest, I had no reason to trust the Word of

God any more than my own feelings and intuitions. That was great when my feelings and intuitions were strong and positive. But on the days when I did not feel God's presence—when God had apparently stopped winking—my feelings became the last thing that I wanted to believe.

So the nagging question for me became, "Is God's revealed and written Word sufficient?" If the answer was yes, then why was I looking for God elsewhere? If the answer was no, then how could I be certain that it was God speaking through my feelings, intuitions, visions, dreams, or all manner of experiences? Might it just be my opinion? Might it be Satan himself?

As Christians, the Lord would not have us constantly wondering what he *might* be up to or what he *may be* saying to us or where he *could be* winking at us. Such a wild-goose chase is only wrought with uncertainty and, ultimately, idolatry. Rather, God gives us certain comfort in what he has *already* promised to do and say. He would have us believe that what he has already promised is enough.

When it comes to our daily lives, the idea that God speaks uniquely and individually to each of us may seem innocent and harmless. But it is precisely that very foundation upon which all false teaching is built—the idea that God has something new to say that he has not spoken to anyone else on earth.

Examples of this abound. You can hear it when a pastor takes the stage and begins a sermon by saying, "God has really laid something on my heart this morning and told me to share it with you." What makes that pastor so different from everyone else? Does he have some different line of communication than we do? Why would God reveal something only to him if it is so important for everyone else to know too? Should I get my pencil and start writing what he says in the blank pages at the back of my Bible? After all, this is apparently God speaking, isn't it?

I have seen YouTube videos of "prophets" who give their viewers God's "word for the week" that he has revealed to them. "This week's word is *worthy*." From this single word the "prophet" will spin a false teaching about how you are supposed to be looking for God to manifest himself in your life this week in new and different ways. All you have to do is tune in to the right divine frequency so you can recognize God when he speaks. So the viewer is sent on a wild-goose chase to find meaning in nearly every interaction or thought they have throughout the week. It would be a shame if the Creator of the universe was trying to talk to you but you missed out because you were not paying attention.

I have even seen people who claim to be Christian pastors engaging in what amounts to tarot card readings, looking for God's message in a spiritual deck of cards. After all, God *could* reveal something there too, couldn't he? Who am I to say he can't? And it is outreach to the mystical pagans to boot.

Other, less blatant examples include people "sensing" that God is leading them to do one thing or another, or God putting a passion in their heart to show them what they ought to do with their life—an interesting idea, given that the Bible never once speaks of our passions in positive terms.

No matter what form it takes, it is always based upon the same premise: God's revealed and written Word is not sufficient, and we require something more from God to know what he is up to. Unfortunately, to look for God in places he has not promised to be found leaves the seeker utterly uncertain and ultimately without true comfort—which is really the thing that makes a person go looking for God in the first place. Where do we find such comfort? How do we respond when someone comes to us claiming to have received a word from the Lord?

I do not have anything new to reveal to you to answer that question; God has not laid anything on my heart to say, nor has he winked at me with some special revelation. But Scripture has plenty to say, so we will stick to that.

Consider the Context

One of the most famous Old Testament prophets was Jeremiah. His commissioning by God and his subsequent skirmishes with false prophets of the day are quite instructive. They teach us how God's people are to respond when someone claims that God is speaking to them.

God comes to Jeremiah and basically says, "You are going to be my prophet to my people" (Jeremiah 1:5). Jeremiah is not so keen on the idea, not because he would be sent to proclaim a very difficult word, but because his youth prevents him from knowing what to say (1:6). However, God reassures Jeremiah by telling him that he will speak what God commands him to speak (1:7). God would give Jeremiah the words to speak, and he seals that promise by touching the prophet's lips (1:9). Isaiah has a similar experience in Isaiah 6:1-7.

If Jeremiah is hesitant to speak because he is afraid of ascribing words to God that God has not actually spoken (the textbook definition of blasphemy), the false prophets he encounters in his ministry are just the opposite. They are happy to put words in God's mouth in an attempt to bring comfort to their hearers. In Jeremiah 23, we are told what makes false prophets false: they claim to speak divine, authoritative words, but God did not give those words to them (23:21-22). So where *did* these false prophets get the words they claim they got from God? From visions of their own minds that provide only vain hopes (23:16), from dreams (23:25), from the deceit of their own hearts (23:26), and, interestingly, from other false prophets (23:30).

Therefore, the people of God were supposed to reject the word of the false prophets. Even though the *content* of their word was quite attractive, as they boldly proclaimed, "No disaster shall come upon you" (23:17), the *source* of their prophecy was wrong. It did not come from God, and therefore was not reliable. The promise sounded great, but there was absolutely no reason to trust it.

Contrast that with the word of God's true prophet, Jeremiah. The people were required to believe his word about exile and judgment, not because it was a message full of roses and rainbows, but precisely because that word was from God himself. If the prophet's word came true, his authority was authenticated. If his word did not come true, he was proven to be false (cf. Deuteronomy 18:22).

This reality hits close to home with the false prophet Hananiah (Jeremiah 28). Hananiah proclaims that all is well and that Israel would spend only a couple of years in Babylonian captivity. Jeremiah actually says that he hopes the prophecy is true. However, God reveals the truth to Jeremiah. When he proclaims that truth to God's people, he also prophesies that

Hananiah would die. Unfortunately for Hananiah, Jeremiah's word came true within the year. He most certainly was sent from God.

One common objection I hear to this is as follows: if God spoke directly to his prophets in the Old Testament, then why can't he speak the same way to us? On the surface it is a fair question. However, there are two things wrong with it. First, nowhere in the Bible does God ever *promise* to communicate to you and me in the same way he communicated to his prophets. When we read the account of his prophets proclaiming the Word he gave them, we are reading a historical narrative—not a paradigm for how God promises to speak to us. Second, now that Christ has come and sent his apostles to record in the Bible the faith "once for all delivered to the saints" (Jude 3), we no longer need God to reveal new things to us. "Long ago," says the author of Hebrews, "at many times and in many ways, God spoke to our fathers by the prophets, but in these last days he has spoken to us by his Son" (Hebrews 1:1-2).

It was not just the Old Testament prophets who had to contend with false teachers. New Testament apostles also defended the sufficiency and authority of their preaching against those who would preach otherwise. Consider the apostle Paul.

Like Jeremiah, Paul had skirmishes with false teachers during his ministry. As a result he had to defend his authority as an apostle. We read an account of this in 2 Corinthians 11. Apparently some so-called "super apostles" had infiltrated the Corinthian congregation and were claiming that they were better than Paul. They criticize him because his writings are heavy, but he himself is absent and his speech is not terribly impressive

(2 Corinthians 10:10). It seems as though the Corinthians had become enamored with teachers that offered something even better than what Paul preached.

After reminding them that he proclaimed the gospel among them free of charge and did not burden anyone with his needs (2 Corinthians 11:7-9), Paul makes an interesting connection. Concerning these false teachers, he says, "For such men are false apostles, deceitful workmen, disguising themselves as apostles of Christ" (11:13). But Paul is not surprised by this: "And no wonder, for even Satan disguises himself as an angel of light. So it is no surprise if his servants, also, disguise themselves as servants of righteousness" (11:14-15). Paul explicitly says that people claiming to be super apostles, claiming to have received direct and new revelation from God, are in fact servants of Satan himself. And yet their word is obviously attractive, for even the Corinthians were taken in by them. (For another example of the same phenomenon, read the book of Galatians.)

I invite you to pause and let it sink in that Satan disguises himself as an angel of light, that he hides his lies in teaching that sounds incredibly true. The fact that Satan so deceives us makes it all the more necessary that we have something objective, certain, and outside of ourselves to which we can cling to know God and his truth.

Satan does not do his work in such a way that, when you see or hear it, you will say, "Oh, hey! There is Satan trying to deceive me." His work will be far more subtle. In fact, he may look just like an angel of light. His words will sound good and true and right, even godly. But his end game is to deceive, kill, and destroy you. He does not care where you are finding comfort

and certainty, so long as it is not the Word of God. He speaks
lies in such a way to have you believe they are from God himself.
Satan would have you on an endless wild-goose chase, searching for God winks, intuitions, gut feelings, warm fuzzies, and
still small voices inside to see what God *might* be saying, rather
than rejoicing in the sufficient, unchanging Word wherein God
has *already* spoken.

If you *think* God *might* be speaking to you some new revelation that you cannot find in the Bible, perhaps a useful litmus
test is this: is it possible that what you are hearing/sensing/feel-
ing could be Satan masquerading as an angel of light in order
to deceive you? If there is the smallest, remotest, tiniest, most
infinitesimal possibility that the answer is yes, then there is absolutely no reason to think that God is the one speaking. In such
instances, we return once again to God's certain and unchanging Word.

Consider the Comfort

There is great comfort to be had when one looks to Scripture
alone for any and all revelation from God. Rather than worrying that we are putting God in a box, we ought to rejoice that
God has put himself in a box. He has condescended to us and
given us an objective way to know exactly where to find him
and his gracious promises.

Consider the comfort this brings when thinking about what
church to attend. The first question we should ask is not, "Do
they have awesome music?" Or "Do they have lots of programs
for the kids?" Or "Are they friendly?" Or "Do I feel comfortable
there?" The first question we ask is this: "Do they preach and

teach God's Word faithfully, constantly placarding Christ crucified and risen for the forgiveness of sins?"

Unfortunately these days, it is not Christ's vision for the church that is preached, but someone else's. It has become popular for the lead pastor to "cast a vision" for the church. The idea is that God gives to this pastor a specific direction or ministry that he wants the church to focus on. It is then the pastor's job to deliver that vision to the congregation and to keep the congregation "on mission," not deviating from this God-given vision.

What ends up happening, whether intentionally or not, is that congregants start following the dreams and visions of a sinful man rather than the objective, knowable mission given by God in his Word. They forget the wisdom of Proverbs 30:5:

> Every word of God proves true;
> he is a shield to those who take refuge in him.
> *Do not add to his words,*
> lest he rebuke you and you be found a liar.

Rather than continuing to teach and preach the unchanging Word of God over and over, they act as if that is boring, as if God has more exciting things to say by giving new visions to church leaders. And in some cases, if those visions are challenged, it is considered tantamount to challenging God himself. Critics who strive to be faithful to the Scriptures get thrown under the bus because they are not on board with the vision God apparently gave to the pastor. Rather than being a servant to Christ's lambs, such a pastor becomes a domineering dictator.

However, the charge that Jesus gives to his church is not secret; it does not need to be revealed to a single man who then passes it along to the rest of the church. Anyone can open the Bible and read exactly what God expects of his church. Not only that, we learn that the direction God gives to his church in the Bible is actually for the sake of our salvation, because it has Christ and his forgiveness at the center.

When we remember that Scripture alone is the place where we learn all that we need to know about God and our relationship to him in Christ, we can be discerning when we hear teaching from a pulpit, stage, book, or Bible study. We can ask, "Is this pastor or teacher or author saying what the Scriptures teach?" We no longer need to be in the uncertain position of being open to what God might be saying through any given medium or endlessly searching for God winks. Rather, we can rejoice in God's comforting truth, which is his Word (John 17:17).

Chapter 17

God Is Proud to Be an American

If my people who are called by my name humble themselves, and
pray and seek my face and turn from their wicked ways, then I will
hear from heaven and will forgive their sin and heal their land.

2 Chronicles 7:14

Consider the Claim

Pastor, do you know the problem with our country today?
We're no longer a Christian nation." It is a comment that I
have heard more times than I would like. A person, usually old
enough to be my mother or grandmother, looks at all the evils
and social degradation in the culture, compares it to the more
pristine and pure time of their younger days, and then concludes that the reason for such moral decay is that "we are no
longer a Christian nation."

The statement assumes at least two things: First, that it is possible for a nation to be "Christian," whatever that might mean; second, that the United States of America used to be such a nation. Being a good Christian and a good American, unfortunately, have become the same thing in the minds of many people. The problem, it is thought, is that we have slowly lost sight of our Christian principles and biblical values. How do we know this? Because people are misbehaving. Or at least they are misbehaving far more than they used to. The answer, then, is to take the advice of God in 2 Chronicles 7:14. If we would just humble ourselves as a nation, if we would pray as a nation, if we would seek God's face as a nation and turn from our wicked ways, only then would God hear from heaven, forgive our nation's sin, and heal our land. Things would finally go back to the way they used to be.

There are two things to consider in this chapter. First, we need to question the assumptions behind the notion of a "Christian nation." Second, we need to consider whether 2 Chronicles 7:14 has something to say about such an idea.

Consider the Context

Have you ever stopped to consider what a Christian nation might look like? What makes a nation (or an individual, for that matter) Christian? Is a Christian nation one that operates according to—or is at least founded upon—biblical principles? Such principles might include the fact that there is a supreme authority, that human beings are valuable and accountable to that authority, and that upright living according to an objective moral standard is beneficial for citizens and the nation as a whole. Now, these things are good as far as they go, but notice that they are not inherently Christian. A Muslim and a Jew could both be agreeable to such principles. Even an agnostic person—who is at least open to the idea of a supreme being—would probably have no problem with these criteria.

So what, then, is Christian about a nation so conceived? The answer, it appears, is nothing. That is the problem with reducing the Bible down to mere principles for living. To do so is to jettison the center and circumference of the Scriptures, namely, Jesus Christ, crucified and risen for the forgiveness of sins. Once a person abandons Christ's own claim that he is the center of the Scriptures, then the door is wide open to make yourself the center of the Scriptures by turning them into nothing more than principles to live by.

So if a nation cannot be Christian based on the principles upon which it is founded, perhaps one might determine a nation's Christianity by looking at the behavior of the citizens. I do not know how many times I have heard something like, "You know, Pastor, in my day people were just nicer. They went to church. Businesses were closed on Sundays. Prayer was allowed in schools, and everyone just seemed to know that everyone else believed in God."

But are any of these things criteria given in Scripture for making a person or institution Christian? The answer, again, is no. Being nice is not what makes a person a Christian. Going to church, though something Christians certainly ought to do (Hebrews 10:24-25), is not what makes a person a Christian. Closing a business on Sunday does not make that business Christian. Praying in school is not necessarily evidence of Christianity (students could be praying to any number of pagan gods, after all). Believing in a generic god is not what makes a person Christian. So, according to these criteria, a so-called Christian nation is just a dream.

But what if you have a right understanding of what it means to be Christian? What if your understanding of a Christian is a person who, by the power of the Holy Spirit, trusts in Christ alone for the forgiveness of all their sins? By this definition, there also is not—nor has there ever been—a Christian nation. At the very least, for such a nation to exist, every single citizen would need to have such faith in Christ—something known only to God. Or perhaps we could use the democratic process: as long as 51 percent or more of a nation's citizens confess faith in Christ, perhaps then we can consider that nation to be Christian.

I hope the problem with the term "Christian nation" is becoming apparent. It is taking the word *Christian*—which can be said only of an individual or a confession of faith—and forcing it upon an institution. It is expecting an earthly nation to be a church.

I am convinced that the reason this phenomenon exists is that it gives us, in our sinfulness, a sense of control and a way to ignore our own wickedness. It fills us with hope that we can save the nation and possibly the world. We do not like the problems we see "out there," and we conveniently focus on them instead of our own sin. We know the problem is that people need Jesus (which is often code for "they need to get their act together"). So the answer is to make our nation Christian again. Get everyone's external lives up to snuff. Then, as a Christian nation, all of our problems will get better. Easy, right? Isn't my nation blessed to have a pious believer such as myself to show them the way?

All they have to do is listen to me. I mean, it's not *that* hard to be righteous like I am. (Please tell me you can sense the sarcasm.)

But what about 2 Chronicles 7:14? Doesn't God tell us there to humble ourselves as a nation, confess our sin, and leave our wickedness behind so that he will heal our land? Well, in short, no, he doesn't.

This verse follows a section of the Bible that describes the dedication of Solomon's grand temple (2 Chronicles 6:1–7:10). The temple—which started as a mobile tabernacle—was a sign of God's grace for his chosen people, Israel. The identity of the nation was intimately bound up with their identity as God's people. To be part of the people of God was to be an Israelite, and to be an Israelite was to be part of the people of God. And what was the center of life for God's people? The temple.

God was present in their midst at the temple, where sacrifices were made daily and blood was shed for sin. The temple's location was also important. It sat within the boundaries of the promised land. It was therefore a constant reminder of God's faithfulness to Abraham, Isaac, Jacob, and all of their descendants. God had promised them a land, and he had made good on that promise. The temple was not for any other nation. It was for Israel, and them alone.

We must keep this in mind, then, when God appears to Solomon and speaks to him. Whatever God says, he says to his chosen people, ancient Israel. He tells Solomon that *his people*—not every nation on earth who live according to his principles—are to humble themselves, pray, seek his face, and turn from their wicked ways, and he would forgive them and heal their land. This exhortation is certainly warranted. After all, Israel had not always been faithful to God. They had grumbled about God's apparent lack of care for them (Exodus 16:1-3), chased after pagan nations' deities (Numbers 25:1-2; Judges 2:17-19; 3:5-6; 1 Samuel 8:7-8), and were not content to have God as their king (1 Samuel 8:4-5). So he is warning them to remain faithful to him, lest they forsake his ways unto destruction.

Second Chronicles 7:14 does not apply to any citizen or nation who happens to be reading it at the time. There is no defensible reason to take these words spoken to ancient Israel and thoughtlessly transfer them to the present day as if God is speaking them now to America. The "land" that God will heal is not any land that just happens to have a Christian living in it. It is specifically the land he promised to Abraham, Isaac, and Jacob (Deuteronomy 34:4). And, in fact, God does heal that land, and so much more. But he does it in a way that is completely unexpected.

Consider the Comfort

God's chosen people, Israel, and the temple that was the center of their life were each only a part of the grand story of salvation that God had set into motion in the Garden of Eden. Even though God chose a single nation to be his beloved and unique people on earth, and even though he put a temple in a specific geographic location to be the center of their worship towards him, it all pointed to someone even greater. Christ himself is the fulfillment of God's people Israel *and* the temple *and* the sacrifices that shaped the temple's life. This is no small thing. For in fulfilling all these things, he opens salvation not only to a single nation but to the entire world.

While the nation of Israel was God's son (cf. Exodus 4:21-23; Hosea 11:1; Matthew 2:13-15) who ultimately failed to heed the warning given to Solomon at the dedication of the temple, Jesus is God's Son who has perfectly kept God's law in their place and ours. While the Old Testament temple worship involved endless sacrifices and the shedding of blood, which ultimately could not atone for sin (Hebrews 10:4), Christ comes as the single, spotless Lamb of God who takes away the sin of the world (John 1:29, 36) and offers himself as the sacrifice that never needs to be repeated (Romans 6:10; Hebrews 7:27; 9:11-12, 25-26; 10:10). Even though the temple in Jerusalem would be razed to the ground (Matthew 24:1-2), Christ is himself the new temple (John 2:18-22), the new holy place where God is present with and for his people, making the former temple obsolete. Christ remarkably comes to save Israel, and simultaneously redefines what it means to be part of Israel, so that Paul can refer to Christians as "the Israel of God" (Galatians 6:16) where "there is neither Jew nor Greek, there is neither slave nor free, there is no male and female, for you are all one in Christ Jesus" (Galatians 3:28).

This may not seem like it has much to do with refuting the idea of a Christian nation, but consider how your citizenship in Christ's heavenly kingdom changes the way you think about your own sin, others' sin, and what your hope is in the midst of that sin. If your citizenship truly is found in Christ, who has made you a child of God by pure grace, then it does not matter at all what nation of the world you happen to reside in.

Additionally, rather than bemoaning everyone else's sin and unrighteousness, your heavenly citizenship is a reminder to you that you own heart is just as wicked and sinful as the next person's (Matthew 15:19-20). Therefore, you can be honest about why the situation in your own country is the way it is. Perhaps when someone asks, "Do you know what the problem with this country is?" our first response should not be, "Yes. The Democratic party," or "Yes. The Republican party," or "Yes. The idiot president," or "Yes. Those potheads living down the street," or "Yes. Those heathen people who hate marriage," or "Yes. Those school shooters who deserve to burn in hell," or "Yes. The greedy men in Washington and on Wall Street." Perhaps when someone asks, "Do you know what the problem with this country is?" our first response should be, "Yes. I am." For when we recognize *that* reality, positing a solution that rests in some hope of a Christian nation is exposed as the foolhardy thing that it is.

Instead of placing our hope in the contrived Christian nation of the past, we rejoice that we *already* belong to a nation that is Christian—a nation that transcends geographical borders, ethnic heritage, languages, tribes, skin color, politics, and even time itself. It is a nation full of saints that have gone before and are now resting from their labors, as well as saints who are presently making the good confession and fighting the good fight all over the globe. And above all, we rejoice that it is a nation for sinners—a nation you have been made a part of by the sheer grace of God in Christ.

Chapter 18

Jesus Came to Make You Rich

I came that they may have life and have it abundantly.

JOHN 10:10

Consider the Claim

It is so cliché these days that we have become almost numb to it when we hear it. Prosperity preaching. It is a stereotype all its own: the singsong voice of the televangelist who is well-groomed and so eloquent that he manages to turn *God* and *Jesus* into three-syllable words; the apparently endless testimonies of everyone who has benefited from their ministry; the refrain of promises like, "Send in your seed offering and God will multiply it to give you the desires of your heart!" and, "God has so much in store for you!" and, "Remain faithful to him, give him all you have, and he will bless you a hundredfold!" Remarkably, even though such preaching has attained a roll-your-eyes, cliché status, millions of people are still drawn to it and subsequently fleeced.

The reason it is so tempting is because it gives hope to the suffering. To be sure, the hope that it offers is false, but it is hope nonetheless—a rare commodity for those in the throes of suffering. Not content with the conundrum that is the suffering believer, the prosperity gospel goes to work solving the problem by promising all manner of well-being for the one who will believe for a miracle, name it and claim it, blab it and grab it, and take for themselves the blessed life that Jesus promises in the here and now.

There is no shortage of biblical texts available to the prosperity preacher. I say that not because the Bible actually teaches a message of worldly prosperity. Rather, what I mean is that there is not a single text in the Bible that the most skilled of them cannot twist into a formula that puts money into their pockets and false promises into your eardrums. So skillful are they in their tactics that they make Harold Hill[5] look like an amateur. They've all got something to sell, and that rhymes with L, and that stands for liars. That's right, I said liars! (Sorry. That was too much, wasn't it?)

The most famous prooftext for the walking Colgate commercial that is the televangelist is John 10:10b: "I came that they may have life and have it abundantly." Jesus is speaking here and his words are obvious, aren't they? It's not as if his words are hard to understand. He comes to give abundant life. Why shouldn't the prosperity preacher promise a great job, a beautiful house, flawless health, a snazzy car, the latest fashion, a perfect spouse, obedient children, fame and friends, with a salary to pay for it all and extra to put away for an early retirement? After all, it seems to have worked for him. So why not me too?

Of course, when people *aren't* experiencing the same sort of blessed success that the televangelist promises, the reason given is that they have not exhibited enough faith and devotion. They have not given enough money. They have not given until it hurts, and so God refuses to bless them.

While there is this cliché version of the prosperity gospel, there is also another, more subtle version of it. The promises held out are not monetary. Rather, the promise is a transformed life. It is the same kind of promise that is embodied in the plot of so many popular "Christian" movies: life is bad, find Jesus, life gets better, and problems cease.

Both the blatant, cliché version of the prosperity gospel and the more subtle version of it are corrected when we consider the sort of abundant life of which Jesus speaks.

Consider the Context

John 10 is one of the most beloved chapters in the Bible. The imagery is beautiful, comforting, and a popular subject of Christian art. Jesus uses the imagery of shepherding. There are those who care for the sheep, and those who do not. The sheep will listen to the shepherd's voice but will flee from the stranger's. The shepherd loves his sheep and will do anything to protect them. The hired hand, however, will save his own skin and leave the sheep when danger approaches. The shepherd exists to give good gifts to his sheep, while the thief comes to steal, kill, and destroy.

These verses, while rightly beloved and cherished, are often considered apart from their context. While of great comfort to us, when Jesus first spoke these words he used them to level judgment upon the religious leaders of the day. The interchange begins all the way back in John 9.

Jesus grants sight to a man born blind (John 9:1-7). It causes quite a stir in the community and they bring the man to the Pharisees. It turns out that the healing occurred on a Sabbath day on which work was prohibited, and so the Pharisees conclude that this Jesus is not from God. If he were, he would not have broken God's law by working on the Sabbath.

This creates a conundrum: if Jesus is not from God on account that he broke the Sabbath, then how do they explain the man standing before them who can now see by the hands of Jesus? Either this Jesus is from God, and therefore lord of even the Sabbath, or else he is performing miracles by the power of demons—a charge that is leveled against him elsewhere (Matthew 9:32-34).

Rather than rejoicing that God is right in their midst, performing miracles to restore his sinful and broken creation, the Pharisees are more concerned that the law has been broken—at least, in their estimation—so they reject the Messiah. In a wonderful turn of phrase, Jesus proclaims that the Pharisees, though they see, are in fact the blind ones (John 9:39-41).

Then Jesus begins to teach in chapter 10 *against* those who would enter the sheepfold apart from the door. The Pharisees were not sent by God to be the religious leaders but were rather self-appointed. I have no doubt that they longed for the Messiah like everyone else, but they refused to accept that Jesus is that Messiah. So they offer people a different sort of religion than the one Jesus brings; they offer a religion of works rather than a religion of mercy and grace. They are the competing voice of the stranger from which Christ's sheep are to flee. They are the thieves and robbers whose teaching will eternally kill and steal and destroy. Out of godly motivation to keep God's commandments, they constructed a fence around the law made up of their own commandments, and then acted as if, by keeping their made-up rules, people could successfully keep God's law and be saved.

Jesus alone, however, comes to bring truly abundant life. Only through him and his work can anyone enter into salvation. He is the *good* shepherd—as opposed to all the lousy ones that have come before. And what does his goodness look like? What is the abundant life that he gives? Well, he tells us. "The good shepherd lays down his life for his sheep" (John 10:11).

The moment Jesus brings up the fact that he will lay down his life for his sheep, his promise of abundant life is filled to the brim with eternal blessings. Jesus did not die so that we would have a plethora of temporal blessings. Jesus died to take our place under the wrath of the one, true, righteous, and almighty God. Christ's death atones for all of our sin, for which we all deserve hell and damnation. Because of Christ, we have true, real, and everlasting life—even when our temporal well-being does not seem so great.

When you consider all that Christ's death and resurrection accomplish for us, the warbling of the televangelist preacher promising health and wealth is exposed for the shallow and empty nonsense that it is. Such preaching robs Christ and his cross of glory and trades it for the cheap wares of the here and now.

Consider the Comfort

Kate Bowler is a thirty-five-year-old wife, mother, Duke professor, and terminal cancer patient. Ironically, she was hurled into the suffering of stage IV cancer while she was researching her dissertation on the history of the prosperity gospel in American religion, now a book called *Blessed* (2013). She has subsequently written *Everything Happens for a Reason: And Other Lies I've Loved* (2018). In her work she reveals the emptiness left by the lies of the prosperity gospel and talks about where her true comfort lies.

In a *Time* magazine interview, Bowler was asked the question, "You are an expert in the history of health, wealth and happiness in American religion. Why do Americans see tragedies as tests of character?" She responded:

> It is one of the oldest stories Americans tell themselves about determination and some supernatural bootstraps. The double edge to the American Dream is that those who can't make it have lost the test or have failed. The prosperity gospel is just a Christian version of that.
>
> *Time* asked, "Did Christianity fail you?"
>
> Sometimes it felt like that, in part because of the stuff people said using the Christian faith to be incredibly trite. Christianity also saved the day. You really want a brave faith, one that says, in the midst of the crushing brokenness, there is the something else there, the undeniable, overwhelming love of God.[6]

Indeed, in the midst of suffering "there is something else there" from which we draw comfort, even when tragedy does not go away. Martin Luther, commenting on the Christian life, writes, "Therefore simply begin to be a Christian, and you will soon find out what it means to mourn and be sorrowful...You will be hindered and hemmed in on every side, so that you will suffer enough and see enough to make your heart sad" (AE 21:20).

He is right, and he is only saying what Jesus himself said. The same Lord who promises to be your good shepherd and lays down his life for you also promises that in this life you will have trouble (John 16:33) and that the world will hate his disciples on account of him (Matthew 10:21-22; 24:9). You have been the victim of the sins of others; you have made others the victims of your own sin. Confessing Christ brings mockery, alienation, and challenges from those who despise him. Like everyone else, your health will fail. Like everyone else, you will struggle at times to make ends meet. Your life, like everyone else, will not be perfect and painless. Put simply, becoming a Christian does not mean life will automatically change and become abundantly better.

And that's okay.

After all, you have the promise of a truly abundant life. You have the promise of life that has been won for you by the good shepherd's death. In the midst of your crushing brokenness, you have a Savior who was crushed and broken for you. You do not have to wonder how you can have *more* faith or sow *more* seed offerings to appease the giant Santa Claus in the sky so that you can get better health, more stable finances, or less stressful relationships. At the end of your life, when your health has finally failed you, you will not be looking back wishing that you had spent more time on the yacht, more money on your car, more time at the gym, or more effort climbing the social ladder. Those things are fine as far as they go, I suppose. But you do not need a crucified Messiah to have them, and they fade even more quickly than they come.

No, when death is staring you in the face, the only thing that will matter to you is the thing that only a crucified Messiah can give: truly abundant life that does not end. Life that is given to you because you could not earn it yourself. Life that you cannot buy. Life that is given through the forgiveness of your sins when the good shepherd bled and died for you and rose again on the third day. Because that abundant life has been given to you, you are truly blessed.

Repeating God's Unchanging Truth

Writing a book concerning misquoted Bible verses carries with it the unique temptation to say things in a way that is novel or profound. I call such a thing a temptation because when it comes to proclaiming and writing about God's Word, we ought to be content to repeat the same unchanging truth that His people have confessed for millennia. Perhaps some of these chapters have sounded quite similar to others. That's okay. The apostle Paul reminded the church in Corinth that he did not speak to them with eloquent, lofty speech or wisdom. He did not come proclaiming anything of his own making, nor was the power in his preaching derived from the world's wisdom or power. Instead, Paul decided to know nothing among them except the apparent foolishness of Christ and him crucified (1 Corinthians 2:1-2). Paul repeated the same message day in and day out to anyone who would listen. While endlessly placarding Christ may seem mundane, boring, and pointless to the world, the church is content to repeat the gospel over and again, for it is the power of God unto salvation (Romans 1:16).

While I have used a variety of approaches to discuss the various Bible verses in this book, I hope that I have not said anything new; that every chapter has clearly proclaimed the same central, life-giving message: that Christ has shed his blood for sinners such as you and me, not because we have earned it, but because of his great love and mercy. Such a glorious promise is the only thing that provides true and lasting comfort in the face of our many trials and temptations. Therefore, let us constantly search the Scriptures and rejoice in the true Savior that they proclaim: Jesus Christ, crucified, risen, and returning for the salvation of the world.

Helpful Terms in Biblical Interpretation

allegorizing—Usually done with parables, to allegorize a text is to take individual pieces and find out what each represents to arrive at a teaching. Christ does this with the parable of the sower. The seed is the word, each different type of soil is a different instance where the word either succeeds in taking root or not, etc. Allegorizing is not always bad, but it can be misused, as in the example of David and Goliath in chapter 14.

Christocentric—To see Christ at the center of a text and the whole Bible.

context—There are primarily two different types of context to consider with a biblical text. First, the literary context, which includes the genre of the text, as well as the surrounding words, sentences, and paragraphs that help us understand the text under consideration. Second, the historical context, which includes the culture, thinking, and practices of a society at a given time period. For example, the context of Corinth in the first century AD was different from the context of Israel in the eighth century BC, which are both different from the context of the United States of America in the twenty-first century AD.

descriptive vs. prescriptive—A descriptive text, often historical narrative, simply conveys an event that happened in history; a prescriptive text commands or prescribes a belief to be held or an action to be performed by Christ's church. For example, the accounts of various biblical characters having multiple wives are descriptive texts. They are not commanding or encouraging polygamy, but rather simply conveying what happened.

eisegesis—The error of putting into a biblical text a meaning that is not there.

exegesis—The discipline of drawing out the meaning of a whole biblical text by understanding the meanings of individual words and how they relate to one another and the surrounding literary context, as well as the historical context.

formal and material principles—To help tease out the finer distinctions between Christian denominations, some will speak about a denomination's *material principle* and *formal principle.* The *material principle* is the central or core teaching of that denomination. The *formal principle* is the source from which that core teaching comes. For example, for Lutherans, the *material principle* is the doctrine of justification by grace through faith in Christ. The *formal principle* is the Bible. Nearly every Christian denomination has the same *formal principle* (i.e., the Bible; the Roman Catholics and Eastern Orthodox also include church tradition and the teaching magisterium of the church as sources of authority). The differences between denominations most often arise in their *material principles.* Calvinists tend to emphasize the sovereignty of God as the central doctrine; Baptists tend to emphasize the exercise of man's will in obedience for conversion as a central doctrine; Roman Catholics place submission to the papacy as a central doctrine; the Orthodox are big on *theosis*, the process of being subsumed into the divine unity and being of God (if I understand it correctly).

hermeneutics—The art of biblical interpretation; a hermeneutic is a set of tools used by an interpreter to arrive at the meaning of a text.

prooftext—A verse or selection of verses used to provide scriptural support for a certain doctrine. For example, John 3:16 is a prooftext for the teaching that Christ died for the world. While using prooftexts is a helpful way to summarize articles of doctrine, one must be careful to avoid simply pulling verses out of their context in order to make a point that the verse, in its context, is not making.

typology—A tool used in hermeneutics that considers the connection between two biblical stories. Typology consists of two pieces. The *type* is the first instance of the story that points to something greater. It is a preview, like the trailer of an upcoming movie. The *antitype* is the second instance that fulfills and surpasses the first. It's the full-length feature. For example, the story of Abraham taking Isaac to the mountain to be sacrificed is the type of Christ's crucifixion outside of Jerusalem—the antitype. The flood of Noah is the type that points forward to the antitype of baptism (1 Peter 3:18-22). Paul speaks of Adam as a type of Christ, the antitype (Romans 5:12-21). The manna in the wilderness (Exodus 16) is a type of Christ, the bread from heaven (John 6). Typology helps us to see the overarching unity of the Holy Scriptures.

Genres of Literature in Scripture

Poetry

- Uses figures of speech in order to make a point
- In English translations, poetry does not usually rhyme
- Examples: the Psalms, Ecclesiastes, Song of Solomon

Prophecy

- When a prophet speaks God's word to his people
- Can be foretelling (declaring what will happen in the future) or forthtelling (declaring what is happening in the present)
- Examples: any of the prophets, Isaiah, Jeremiah, Ezekiel, Daniel, Elijah, Elisha

Narrative

- Tells a story

- Told from the perspective of the narrator

- Examples: Genesis, Exodus, 1 and 2 Samuel, 1 and 2 Kings, 1 and 2 Chronicles, the Gospels, Acts

Parable

- A common story that illustrates a deeper point

- Most often told by Jesus

- Examples: the parable of the sower (Matthew 13:3-23), the parable of the unforgiving servant (Matthew 18:21-35), Nathan's confrontation of David (2 Samuel 12:1-15)

Didactic

- Doctrinal teaching

- The author or speaker presents information that he wants the readers to know and believe

- Examples: Christ's sermon on the mount (Matthew 5–7), Paul's letters, Peter's letters

Apocalyptic

- Teaching about the end times
- Highly symbolic or figurative and therefore difficult to interpret
- Examples: Revelation, sections of Daniel, some of Christ's teaching

Questions to Ask When Reading a Biblical Text

1. What genre of literature is it?

2. What is the context before the text and after?

3. If there is dialogue, who is speaking and who is hearing?

4. Who/what are the antecedents of the pronouns? Are the pronouns singular or plural?

5. Is the text descriptive or prescriptive?

6. What is the law in the text? What is the gospel in the text?

7. How is the text Christocentric?

8. What moves are you making to apply the text to our modern context? (For example, are you automatically assuming every "you" in the text is referring to you personally? If so, why are you making that move? Are you allegorizing a story and extrapolating meaning that is not there (e.g., the story of David and Goliath)? If so, why are you making that move?

Endnotes

1. *Lutheran Service Book* (St. Louis, MO: Concordia Publishing House, 2006), 265.

2. A very helpful discussion of this distinction can be found in a sixteenth-century Reformation document called the Formula of Concord. The section dealing with mankind's will is Article II.

3. A *talent* was a large unit of currency. While the value varied over time, on average a single talent could be worth around twenty years of wages. Consider this and do the math the next time you read the parable of the unforgiving servant in Matthew 18:23-35.

4. An interesting dynamic happens when the church gets involved with the culture's social justice wars. When we flap our mouths about every single social ill that Fox News or CNN would have us outraged about, we simply become one tiny little squawk in a sea of outrage. Then when we actually try to speak the gospel—the single message on the planet that *only* the church can proclaim—the world around us simply says, "Oh, them? They are spouting off about something else again? Oh, well." The church would do well to be picky about which societal issues are worth her words, so as not to lose the "purchase price," if you will, of the gospel.

5. Harold Hill is a con man and traveling salesman in the 1962 musical comedy *The Music Man.*

6. Elizabeth Dias, "Kate Bowler Talks About Her Cancer Diagnosis and Her Faith," *Time*, January 25, 2018, http://time.com/5118044/kate-bowler-interview-cancer-faith/.

To learn more about Harvest House books and
to read sample chapters, visit our website:

www.harvesthousepublishers.com

HARVEST HOUSE PUBLISHERS
EUGENE, OREGON